The
Angel
Messages

Copyright © 2003 Jenny Boylan

First printed in the U.S.A. under the title
The Angel Messages. ISBN: 1 4010 5893 0 (hardcover) and
ISBN 1 4010 5892 2 (softcover)

This reissue © 2003 O Books
46A West Street, Alresford, Hants SO24 9AU, UK
Tel: +44 (0) 1962 736880 Fax: +44 (0) 1962 736881
www.0-books.net

US office:
240 West 35th Street, Suite 500
New York, NY 10001
E-mail: obooks@aol.com

Design by Nautilus Design

ISBN 1 903816 23 8

A CIP catalogue record for this book is available from the British Library.

Printed in the USA by Maple-Vail

The
Angel
Messages

Jenny Boylan

BOOKS

New York, USA
Alresford, UK

Dedication

This book is dedicated to:
Felicia, my favorite angel, in loving memory of the first Angel
message book we created together.
My mom, for always believing in my work and in the Angel
messages . . . I love you!
And for all the other angels, who without your support, my life
would not be the living miracle it is today: Spirit, Jerome, Master
Wu, Daniela, Ketmala, Billy, Laura, Amy & John, Leslie, Pat,
Frank, Katie, Tom, Enrique, Amy M., Melody, Shila and family,
Christy, Staci and Debbie.
A special thanks to my editor, Samantha . . . you turned greatness
into excellence!

About the Cover

S ometimes angels are in our lives and we never see them. Other times, angels gift to us a glimpse of their presence. These gifts become a treasure which impacts each of us in a special way. The angel picture on the cover was taken by my friend, Ketmala, while visiting an arboretum in Pennsylvania. At the time she took the picture, she found the water fountains to be particularly beautiful, however, it was not until after it was developed and shared with a friend that the angel was actually noticed.

One day, I shared my copy of Ket's angel picture with a client who was battling a severe experience with cancer. The cancer had spread aggressively throughout his body leaving him with numbered days. When he saw the angel picture, he started crying. After some time, he dried his eyes and thanked me for sharing it with him. He told me that a few hours before my visit, he had prayed to the Universe to give him a sign that life existed after death. Feeling alone and afraid of his impending death, he wanted reassurance that he would be okay. When he saw this picture, a deep, peacefulness and profound gratitude filled him while leaving a lasting impression on each of us in the room with him at the time.

Thank you Ket, for sharing this special picture with all of us and thank you to the angel who graced us with her presence.

Introduction

One of the most common questions each soul encounters on its journey to spiritual awareness is this: Can life ever go back to being normal? The question which rarely follows, though, is this: If it could, would you want it to return to normal?

When you were young, life stretched out before you as a straight and open road. You had dreams about what you wanted to be when you grew up, where you wanted to live and even dreams of finding love. Perhaps you never allowed yourself to dream at all, believing the status quo of your life circumstances were to become your ultimate destiny. Rarely did thoughts arise of intersecting roads or detours. However, when these intersections undoubtedly appeared, your days were spent focused in reflection of your past as you wondered if your life would ever be normal again. Time and energy were spent on questions of "what ifs" and "why's" rather than on "what could be now". You yearned for a past which no longer existed and became stuck in a present of unhappiness mixed with fleeting moments of joy. Perhaps your past was not enjoyable, so you shifted your focus to dreaming of a better future while doubting its potential existence. Then, when a good day arrived, you held on tightly, fearful . . . for your past experiences had taught you not to trust that anything good would last... which only compounded your struggles.

Through the culmination of experiences, your life became an eternal search for security in a secure-less world. The desire to place your trust in the world around you served only to add levels of structure to an already faulty foundation . . . where the end result could only be collapse. Your choices were twofold: You could wait until the eventual collapse and have Spirit step into your life or you could choose to invite Spirit into your life first, releasing the need for security altogether.

Life was never meant to be secure or normal, especially a normal as it is defined by others who are living in fear . . . fear they will never be loved or touch the passion of their souls. Life was and is meant to be a living miracle. All experiences have been designed to awaken you to this miracle. To the extent you embrace this truth readily and integrate it into your daily experiences, moments for incredible transformation shall arise. No longer needing security, your craving will be life, a deeply abundant one. Instead of a destiny of status quo, your destiny will manifest as a promise of joy and love, as the voice of your soul beckons you to new places . . . to new horizons... to the unknown. You will leave normal, never able to return, but Spirit promises . . . you will never want to.

These Angel messages are reminders of Spirit's promise to turn a routine life into a miraculous one. They have been written for those times you become lost on the path of creating your life dreams; when you need a resource for inspiration; when you want to step back into the flow of life; and best of all, when you want to celebrate your feelings of joy. While conveying all is possible, they remind you that challenges are opportunities in disguise and limitations are only perceived . . . soul-lutions are always present. Assisting you with remembering how powerful you truly are, they re-connect you with your spirit confirming what your heart already knows to be true: You are potential made manifest.

It is my intention to offer you friendship through this collection of Angel messages, a friendship which will always be there for you no matter the experience. Trust fully that whenever you open this book, to whatever page, you will be deeply guided, inspired and empowered to create and live the life of your dreams. These messages were written for you . . . to echo the voice of your soul whenever you choose to listen. May you also share these Angel messages with loved ones, offering them a treasure to let them know you believe in them, in their dreams and in their potential to make their deepest wishes come true.

Now . . . go to your destiny.

Message from the Angel of Joy

Were we to find joy in the moment and allow it to become an everlasting moment, we would opt out of the drama of daily life.

Message from the Angel of Expression

When you arrive at a crossroads in life with tears streaming down your face, understand that your tears are not for sadness or for joy, but for fear you cannot walk the path your soul has chosen. Your tears are for the relationships you had to leave in your desire to live truthfully . . . and for those who have turned away from you not yet ready to see the truth within their hearts. Your tears are for those times the truth revealed itself only to have you turn your gaze away fearing even greater losses.

Why, though, do you give more power to your fear of the truth when your heart yearns deeply to live it? Simply, it is because the truth means death . . . the death of the illusion you call your life and the death of your perceived safety in illusion. Something greater beckons you forward. By walking the path your soul has chosen, the ultimate truth will reveal itself... the truth is not that your soul has chosen a path, but you have chosen to be.

Message from the Angel of Closure

We spend a great portion of our lives looking for closure within our experiences . . . from needing to know why a certain relationship ended, to needing assurance about the outcome of our choices. Our fear of the unknown need not create the anxiety we currently allow it. If we were to focus our attention toward sustaining a deeper relationship with our soul, the sense of inner peace we seek would pervade our every experience. So, do not seek to bring closure to your life experiences, but seek to bring closure to the current gap which exists between you and your eternal essence.

Message from the Angel of Destiny

You ask to be shown your destiny and Spirit lights the path before you . . . as you look away.

You pray to live your passion and Spirit opens the floodgates within your heart . . . as you squelch it back down.

You cry out for meaning in your life and Spirit connects you with the voice of your soul . . . as you close your ears to the sound of it.

Then, when you fall to your knees in despair wondering why Spirit has abandoned you as the sound of silence echoes, remember this . . .

It is not that Spirit has abandoned you, rather Spirit has stepped back until you commit to answering destiny's call with the full knowledge that nothing is going to stop you.

Destiny is never handed to you on a plate, but held on a plate before you . . . a plate for which you must choose to reach.

Message from the Angel of Love

When all is said and done, the final question will not be Were you loved? The final question will be how you loved those who were in your life, including those who briefly crossed your path.

Message from the Angel of Success

Within each person's heart lies a seed of belief that they have
failed in some way. Whether it is a large or small failure matters
not. All that truly matters is what is taken from the failed
experience and how wisdom gained is applied in an empowered
way to any and all future experiences.

Message from the Angel of Life

To live with regret is one thing; to use it as an excuse for living is quite another.

Message from the
Angel of Joy

Ask Spirit what your calling is in this lifetime and Spirit will
reply, "It is the greatest calling of all . . . to live joyfully."

Message from the Angel of Magnificence

Every time you respond to life with "I 'can't'" or "but," you miss an opportunity to experience your own magnificence.

Message from the
Angel of Passion

When the fire of your soul ignites the passion within your heart,
do not view it as an opportunity for success or failure, but view it
as an open door for miracles.

Message from the Angel of Impermanence

In our endless search to create a life of permanence within the illusory physical world experience, we overlook the miraculous beauty of our soul's true nature . . . that of impermanence.

Were we to, instead, embrace our soul's everlasting essence, we would find life's daily struggles disappear only to be replaced by incredible joy.

Message from the Angel of Perception

You can look at your life and think that this is your lot, or you can view your lot in life as the raw material needed to make your life the work of art it was meant to be.

Message from the Angel of Authenticity

You can live your life trying to be someone that other people like. And of course, you can live your life living up to what you perceive as another person's expectations of you and for you. But both of these life focuses will only create feelings of frustration and disappointment.

There is, however, another option. You can live your life for you and you can like who you are by living true to your deepest feelings and inspirations. It is this very focus and way of life that creates the feelings of joy and love that you seek.

Message from the Angel of Observations

We expand and live to our fullest creative potential whenever we practice having first thoughts that reflect *observations* rather than *conclusions* about any and all life experiences, whether they be our own experiences or those of a stranger.

Message from the Angel of Greatness

At some point in each person's life, they will be tested in their call to greatness. Those that pass the test will be the ones that don't meet anger with anger, but instead, rise above the anger and respond with love and in wisdom.

Message from the
Angel of World Peace

Standing there, you point your fingers at us in blame . . . as the
bombs explode around you.

Standing here, we point our fingers at you in blame . . . as people
die around us.

All this time, while we point fingers at one another, we never
once paused to reflect on our own accountability for the events
that have occurred. It is not the leaders who are solely responsible
for any world event, but it is each of us, the parts that make up
the whole, that are *soul-ly* responsible for each and every world
event . . . for the events that have occurred and for those whose
time has yet to come.

We are accountable for our indifferences towards the world
around us as much as we are accountable for our passion to make
a difference. In the end, whenever we choose as a collective group
for that end to arrive, the fingers that we have pointed in blame
at one another or at other nations really will not matter one single
bit if there is no one left to see them.

Choose world peace now.

In memory of September 11, 2001.

26

Message from the Angel of Worry

"It's difficult not to worry," you say. But isn't it actually the worrying that makes life difficult?

Message from the Angel of Love

When tragedy or disaster occurs in the world involving global centers of power, tap into and utilize your creative potential by holding the highest vision, centered in love, of all world leaders. It is in holding these high visions that you facilitate the leaders' alignment with their spirit... not their ego . . . in any subsequent actions to the tragedy or disaster. It is the energy of love that ultimately heals and it is the power of love, the only authentic power, which supports and sustains us through the greatest of challenges.

Message from the Angel of Awareness

How many times in your life have you stopped what you were doing to marvel at the beauty of a rainbow? In all your marveling, have you ever paused to understand how exactly a rainbow is created? Using the rainbow as a starting point, how many other experiences in your life do you witness without pausing to look deeper into understanding why or how they are created? Looking at life with this greater awareness does not lessen its beauty. A greater awareness of life only enhances your understanding of the miraculous creation process underlying it.

Message from the Angel of Change

As it has been said before, the one constant in life is change. Since this is a true statement and you know there is nothing that you can do to stop it, then why do you continue to resist it? Don't try to stop change, but instead, stop the practice of labeling the experiences of change as either good or bad. Labeling your experiences causes your discomfort, your pain, not the experience itself. In addition, the labeling only furthers your resistance to the present moment. So take a deep breath, trusting the fact that your experience will soon change into another experience and then into yet another experience as the process of life, the process of your life, continues to unfold . . .

Message from the Angel of Essence

There will always be experiences in which you receive something that you think you want only to feel disappointed when it actually arrives. These feelings of disappointment arise due to one thing and one thing only: Lack of clarity about the essence of what it is you are seeking to create within your life experiences. Experiences are only the package in which essence is delivered. Instead, strive for clarity of mind regarding the essence of the experiences that you want to create in your life, rather than focusing on the package in which it is delivered. Only then will you create deep, lasting joy and abundance.

Message from the Angel of Manifestation

The effortless manifestation of your life dreams begins with you and the 4 C's of the creative process:

Clarity: Be clear and focus on what you want to create rather than focusing on what you don't want to create. Remember that what you focus on expands and what you don't focus on contracts.

Conscious Creation: Consciously keep empowered thoughts and beliefs in your mind. When speaking about yourself and your life, choose your words with the utmost care and love while allowing your actions to be aligned with your empowered Self.

Commitment: The achievement of your goal is assured the moment you commit yourself to it.

Co-Passion: Align your passion with the passion of your soul and allow the energy of this union to open you to your potential and to the realm of possibilities.

Message from the Angel of Leadership

A headstrong leader lives life with passion and commitment. But it is only when a leader lives life with passion, commitment and Spirit that true leadership manifests.

Message from the Angel of Abundance

Living life at the survival level is not a reflection of your Divine essence. If you find yourself living at this survival level, whether it is financially, emotionally or spiritually, recognize it as a transformational opportunity. Then to complete the transformation from poverty consciousness to abundant thinking, call on the energy of your spirit. For it is your spirit that has been absent from your experiences all this time.

Message from the Angel of Spirit

Calling back your spirit now.
No longer afraid.
Your face wet with tears, tears that once only wept silently within
the confines of your heart.
Your purpose in the past . . . left unfulfilled.
A purpose, this time, to be lived . . . and completed.
Calling back your spirit now.

Message from the Angel of Light

As bright as the light of a candle in a darkened room, your spirit shines. But without oxygen, a candle's flame ceases to exist. Like the flame, without the energy of your soul, your spirit's light also flickers out.

Message from the Angel of Soul

"Take me with you on this journey," beckons the soul. "I am the force behind your thoughts and the power behind your love. With me, attuned to Spirit, all is possible."

Message from the Angel of Joy

Why is it with pain that you draw closer to Spirit? Do you not know that Spirit can also be found in joy?

Message from the Angel of Passion

When your passion stirs within you, what do you do? As your passion builds, unleashing itself from the confines of your heart, do you answer its call to action? When it pulsates through every fiber of your being, do you give it full expression? What is it that scares you so about your passion? After all, it is only the call of *your* spirit, the power of *your* soul, and the whisper of Divine Love. To deny it is to deny your very essence. Answer its call . . . for yourself . . . and for those who also need the inspiration to answer their passion's call. What you believe you are doing only for yourself, you are also doing for others.

Message from the Angel of Dreams

Each night, the light of the stars shines brightly down upon the dreams that lie within you. But unlived dreams are like an unlived life. Rather than settling for the light of the stars to shine down upon you, resolve today to let your dreams loose. Let them carry you on their back up to touch the face of the stars as your dreams take flight.

Message from the
Angel of Relationships

Did you know that you are an author? It's true. You are the author of your own life story, even though your novel may not yet be finished. The title of your story is: "The Life of _____". (Hint: You fill in the blank.) Interestingly, the characters in your novel, beginning from day one, are not quite who you thought them to be. For example, until now you may have been viewing many of your relationships with your friends, family and partner as personalities. Some of these personalities you like, perhaps even love, and some of them you struggle to like at all. A few of these personalities may be your greatest source of joy or greatest point of frustration. But, whether you like or dislike the personality, one thing is guaranteed: When you view each person in your life as a fellow soul, a soul that perhaps lost itself in its personality, your perspective on any and all of your experiences with these souls can be greatly expanded towards love, compassion and forgiveness. Now, instead of a life story centered on struggle, it can be focused on the greatest adventure there is: Life.

Message from the Angel of Happiness

So many times we believe that we cannot be happy until a certain something or someone arrives into our life. Choosing to put off our happiness in this way however, is not the best choice that we can make. The better choice is in choosing to be happy now. This way when that certain something or someone finally does arrive, you will be in a great mood to receive them.

Message from the Angel of Personal Power

Why do you believe that it is so challenging to step into your personal power? It does not have to be, if you remember who you are. Choose to know this Truth about yourself. Choose opportunities and possibilities, *knowing* that everything is possible. Do not believe in limitations. Choose to believe in possibilities then apply your choices across the board of life. Not here or there, but across the board. You are not powerful only in certain situations; you are powerful in all situations. You are a force to be reckoned with. You can make any and all changes in any area of your life that you choose. But first, you *must choose.*

Message from the Angel of Dreams

When you focus on living your deepest dreams and the challenge
to live them seems too great, do not give up. Instead, take a
moment to connect with the power of your spirit. Imagine that it
is like a silver cord that reaches up and out of your heart
attaching itself to the brightest star in the sky. Then, when the
temptation to give up arises, hold on tight with all your might,
remembering that the process of achieving your dreams is equally
as important as the dream itself.

Message from the Angel of Strength

Challenges are in your life to show you where you already have strength and to help you identify areas where you are developing greater strength.

Message from the
Angel of Promise

To reflect back onto your life and think that you *could have* done
something differently only means that the experience at the time
was not what you wanted. Or, to reflect back onto your life and
think that you *would have* done something differently means that
your experience and your choice were reflective of your personal
growth at the time. Instead of living life with *could haves* and
would haves, and berating yourself for past choices, look at your
life today and ask: "What do I want to create for my life now and
what choices do I need to make today to bring these creations to
me?" This way you will not be living focused on past regrets,
instead, you will experience the fullness of the present moment
and be open to receive the promise of tomorrow.

Message from the Angel of Self-belief

The opportunity to believe in yourself is always a greater challenge than the familiar choice of self-doubt. It is within the realm of possibility that you will eventually grow weary of your self-doubt, so much so, that the challenge of self-belief becomes a welcome change.

Message from the Angel of Action

There comes a time when you need to stop talking about life and instead, start living it.

Message from the Angel of Solution

Do not search within your heart for whom to blame for your lot in life, but search within your heart for the solution to rise above it.

Message from the Angel of Light

Do not seek to know your shadow side. You already spend enough time thinking about it or being harsh with yourself because of it. Choose today, instead, to embrace your light side.

Message from the Angel of Spirituality

Life, when lived spiritually, focuses on creating love, joy and abundance. In fact, with a spiritual life focus, struggle disappears altogether. So why, then, do you question life as a spiritual process? Or, if you believe that life is a spiritual process, why do you struggle to live it with a daily commitment? The struggle with your full belief or complete commitment to your spirituality can often be found in this simple statement: You question the existence and value of that which cannot be seen with your eyes.

Within the ocean depths, life forms of every imaginable shape, color and size exist in abundance. Even though you cannot see them when looking at the ocean from your viewpoint, they still exist. When it comes down to the very air that you breathe, you cannot see it yet it, too, exists. Like the ocean and like the air that you breathe, spirituality exists. So instead of living your life according to what is perceived by your eyes or verified by science, live it aligned with the truth in your heart and you will truly create the love, joy and abundance that are your natural birthright. After all, aren't these the very qualities you seek to attain in life with or without spirituality? At least now your chances of success are assured.

Message from the Angel of Spirit

All this time, it has pretended to be your friend, telling you not to take risks so that you would not appear foolish. "Do this," it said, so that others approved of you. At a great cost, you have listened to it while your spirit suffered. No more. Bid it farewell. Today set your spirit free. No longer concerned about what others may think, you follow your spirit wherever it leads. Spread your wings for all to see. You are free to be you now ... and more. Good-bye, ego. May your ego's path and your spirit's path never cross again.

Message from the Angel of Self-love

A life filled with self-love results in fewer difficulties. So why, then, is self-love not a priority in your life? Most likely it is because you simply do not understand the inherent potential within self-love to transform struggle into joy. But an opportunity now presents itself to you to do exactly this. Now you can shift your understanding into the realization that difficulties in life arise from a lack of self-love. It is not that a life with self-love is difficult to live; rather, it is a life without self-love that is difficult.

Message from the Angel of Surrender

Reaching a surrender point never means surrendering your ability to make a choice. When you surrender your ability to make a choice, you are attempting to avoid responsibility for your situation. Genuine surrender means that you have arrived at a point where the options before you seem inadequate or incomplete for what you want to create in your life. Your role then, at this moment, is to step back and reflect on what it is that you truly want to create. Then, surrender the details of how that can be created over to Spirit, trusting that options, which before were unknown, will become known and available to you.

Message from the Angel of Abundance

Do not ask for security in life, ask for abundance. Security means that someone or something is your source which results in a fear of losing that source. Abundance, however, is a state of being that stays with you through every experience. There is no fear of loss since you know that you, the Divine part of you, are the source.

Message from the Angel of Joy

Today, stop for a moment and ask yourself how many times you hold yourself back from doing something fun and spontaneous because you wonder what someone else will think. Next time you are out and about, observe the children who cross your path. Watch how they play so freely. Notice the adults' expressions that pass by them. Chances are that the adults watching them have a warm smile on their face. There is something both comforting and inspiring to watch a person, no matter the age, be so alive and full of joy. Remember this the next time you are tempted to hold yourself back from living the moment fully and freely.

Message from the Angel of Awareness

Answers may come in all forms, but they will not help you unless you are aware of the questions that go with them. The only way to know the questions is through self-awareness.

Message from the
Angel of Self-Acceptance

Next time you find yourself defending or explaining your life, life experiences or behaviors to another, know that it is not the other person who is uncomfortable with you. It is you who is uncomfortable with you. Reflect on this discomfort so that you can move into self-acceptance. Through self-acceptance you create deep inner peace.

Message from the Angel of Expression

When you emulate another person, remember that it is not that they have something that you do not have. Instead, these experiences are opportunities for you to identify and cultivate these same qualities that lie dormant within you.

Message from the Angel of Self-Acceptance

Why do we become upset when we feel that someone is putting us down? If we were to listen to our daily inner dialogue, we would recognize that this person is only reflecting what we do to ourselves every day. The moment, though, when we choose to stop putting ourselves down and to accept ourselves fully, so will others.

Message from the Angel of Truth

It is only in silence that Truth emerges. This may explain why we always make so much noise in our lives. We fear the Truth, our Truth, because of the changes we may be required to make in our lives. Running from our Truth, though, is never a good solution. Today, take time to embrace the silence and listen for the whispers of your Truth within it.

Message from the Angel of Potential

Because we fear disappointment, we often avoid situations that could result in these feelings. Yet, through our avoidance, we experience the very thing we sought to avoid in the first place, while we miss out on all our potential for joy. Put this way avoidance is not really working for us, is it?

Message from the Angel of Communication

Many times in our conversations with others, we worry about what we say and how it will be perceived. Such a focus limits our freedom of expression while conveying a disempowered egoist message. Think about this for a moment: If we, instead, choose to hold a higher vision of those we converse with, we create a space for them with which to respond to that higher vision.

The next time you find yourself focusing on someone's reaction to your spoken thoughts, shift the conversation up a gear. Rather than talking to their ego or personality, talk to their soul. There is nothing more fulfilling than a soul-to-soul connection.

Message from the Angel of Intuition

Always go with your intuition in every situation rather than your ego. How can you be sure, though, which is which? Your ego is attached to the outcome of your choice and your intuition reflects a deeper feeling of "rightness" ultimately leading to an excellent outcome.

Message from the
Angel of Support

So you feel abandoned by Spirit, do you? Or maybe, you feel unloved by the Universe? Realize that this isn't your soul talking. It is your ego. Sometime during your journey through life, your ego's need was not met. You interpreted that experience as a form of abandonment. The problem with this interpretation is that it is holding you back from living your life now.

You have so much incredible potential to take your life to new heights, but you cannot realize this potential when you are busy sulking over perceived past grievances. Give your ego a hug and then a good solid kick to get it going. You have a life waiting for you out there and a Universe wanting to support you. Come on now, you can do it.

Message from the Angel of Life

How often do we hear the expression, "It's not bad once you get used to it?" Life is not about getting used to something. It is about living it fully. No exceptions.

Message from the Angel of Simplicity

Rules for Living:

Be free . . . be yourself.
Live life, love life.
Go the distance. Always.

Simple is always better!

Message from the Angel of Communication

If you ever find yourself in a situation with loved ones who are struggling with a problem, never rush in and attempt to fix it. This only communicates that you believe them to be incapable of doing so themselves. Instead, offer your love and emotional support. In the long run, this will go a lot further than any short-term fixes. Not to mention the message that it communicates to them is a powerful one . . . the message being that you believe in them . . . fully.

Message from the
Angel of Sacrifice

In any relationship, should you ever catch yourself thinking that you are giving up a lot for someone, pause and take a moment to reflect. This thought indicates a need to better understand your intentions when making choices. Without this understanding, there could be much resentment down the road, resentment that you can do without.

Looking at your situation, now, notice that you are not giving up something for someone else. You are giving up something for you. To pretend otherwise and believe that you are doing it for someone else is unhealthy and only leads to conflict later on. Now, the next question that begs to be asked is this: "Why do you want to believe that you are doing what you are doing for another and not for yourself?" Herein lays a wonderful opportunity for personal growth.

Message from the Angel of Courage

Sometimes courage means being able to walk away from something that no longer serves you rather than just grinning and bearing it.

Message from the Angel of Dreams

Everyone has a dream and everyone knows what they want at some level of their being. It is just that not everyone believes that they can have what they want or they think that they need permission first to receive it. But the truth is . . . dreams come true the moment you believe they do . . . and that is all there is to it.

Message from the Angel of Passion

Passion is living for what you love to do and never settling for anything less than that.

Message from the Angel of Hope

Feelings of hope arrive when you fear allowing yourself to *know* that you can create what you want for your life. Hopeful feelings suggest an opportunity is present for you to engage your spirit in your experience while releasing all expectations of what the outcome *should* look like, but trusting the outcome will be awesome.

Message from the Angel of Life

There are times when life presents you a choice to make all your dreams come true. One option will be passion with no known outcome, the other: joyless financial security. One of these options makes the heart swell with joy while the other acts like a cage for the soul. When this choice presents itself and fear feels like your companion, make the choice your spirit guides you to make and hold on just a bit longer... your dreams are just around the corner.

Message from the Angel of Success

When people are not happy or supportive of your success, do not take it personally. Your success makes it glaringly obvious to others that they are holding themselves back. When you arrive at this point, you must remain strong. Your success, now, is not just for yourself, it is for all of mankind.

Message from the Angel of Honesty

Honesty in our relationships only exists when we are honest with ourselves. Without self-honesty, our life becomes a lie of our own creation.

Message from the
Angel of Choice

To feel sad about a situation that arises unexpectedly is one thing, but to feel sad about a situation where you have a choice, is quite another. Realize, my friend, you always have a choice. Even if it is only in choosing how you wish to respond to unexpected situations.

Message from the Angel of Beliefs

Each day society bombards you with untruths and false beliefs concerning every area of life. Choose with utmost care which beliefs you take into yourself as truths and in which you invest your spirit. Beliefs, after all, are the pivotal basis of your reality.

How do you like your reality so far?

Message from the Angel of Truth

Ignorance is an eye turned blind to the Truth. What exactly, then, is it about the Truth that you fear, so much so, that you need to turn your eyes blind towards it?

Message from the
Angel of Nurture

If you believe that you have no value unless you are taking care of everyone else other than yourself, realize that it is only your ego motivating your actions. Your spirit knows that it can only truly nurture others when it has been nurtured first.

Message from the Angel of Choice

In moments of indecision, taking the easy way out is never the best choice. Moments of indecision are opportunities to create greater clarity about what you want and then to make the necessary choices accordingly.

Message from the Angel of Rest

How we approach rest is indicative of how we approach life. This means that if we approach rest only when we are fully exhausted, we are not honoring the flow of life, but pushing ourselves too hard. Approaching rest with a sense of boredom suggests that rest may not be what we need and that life is calling us to do something else. We, again, are not honoring the flow of life. The best approach to life is with a full sense of awareness of where and what our spirit is calling us to do . . . and then doing just that.

Message from the Angel of Health

The body speaks with pain only when you have not addressed its whispers for love and attention.

Message from the Angel of Leadership

A true leader never views herself as a leader, but as a champion of dreams to those that surround her. Her first order of business is not to tell you what she thinks you should do, but to ask you what you want to do and then support you through the process of making it happen. This is leadership at its finest.

Message from the Angel of Expectations

We are so busy living up to external expectations that we forget our internal expectations. Scarier still, due to the disconnection within ourselves, we can no longer tell the difference between them. The solution: Take some time today and reconnect with your inner self.

Message from the Angel of Humility

A false humility is just as bad as an untamed ego. Genuine humility occurs when you own your value without the need to flaunt it for external validation.

Message from the Angel of Responsibility

You are responsible for your intentions in all interactions and it is your responsibility to align this intention with your spirit. You are *not* responsible for how another person chooses to perceive your intentions. When you make yourself responsible for others in this way, you greatly diminish their potential as capable and competent people.

Message from the Angel of Miracles

It is not that we question the miracles we are shown in life. It is that we fear what the miracles call us to do.

Message from the Angel of Surrender

When standing at the crossroads and confusion overwhelms you, while fear paralyzes your forward step, take a deep breath. Then surrender your will to your soul. Now the best path, that until this moment had remained unseen, can reveal itself.

Message from the Angel of Leadership

What value is there in your talk, when you are called to action and fail to walk it?

Message from the Angel of Character

Seek neither fame nor glory, but rather seek a depth of character that sustains the fame or glory when it arrives.

Message from the Angel of Dreams

Go past the "reality" of your life and find your dream. See your life through the eyes of a child not yet encumbered with limitations. Then make your life the masterpiece it was meant to be. After all, "reality" is only a limitation you place on your life when you are afraid to live your dreams.

Message from the Angel of Success

Your success in life is not measured by wealth, career or relationships. Your success in life is measured by how much you love yourself, including:

Who you have been in the past, who you are today, and who you are becoming.

Message from the
Angel of Life

You can either wait until things are different before you start living or you can decide to fully participate in life now. Waiting for things to be different is playing it safe at the game of life and this keeps you from really living. Make the choice of how you want to live life now and then show up for it . . . for all of it . . . for the good and the bad.

Remember, you cannot change the past, but the past has led you to this moment, a moment to make life anew.

Message from the Angel of Spirit

In any situation, when you become aware that your ego is seeking validation, choose to release this need. Instead, come from your spirit with the intention of being of service to another soul in whatever way your spirit leads you.

Message from the
Angel of Inner Knowing

Your spirit is like the sun. There will be days when you look into the sky and can view the sun in all its brilliance. There will also be days when the sun is blocked by clouds or a storm. However, you know that the sun is still in the sky. Remember this inner knowing when the clouds or the storms of struggle move into your own life and when the thought of connecting to your spirit seems an impossible feat.

Message from the Angel of Release

To suffer or not to suffer . . . is that the question? Why not release the belief that you need to suffer and open your heart to Love? Love can transform your life in countless ways. Love makes each day special and filled with an abundance of miracles. But first, you must invite Love in while opening your heart to receive It.

Message from the
Angel of Joy

Absoul-lutely everything you need to feel joyful lies within. When joy arises from the depths of your being, pulsating through every cell; when you cannot stop smiling, even if you try; and when you want to shout at the top of your lungs how much you love life even though there are still challenges, know this: This joy is always there for you to tap into whenever you choose.

Message from the
Angel of Divine Guidance

There is a loving Presence that flows through your life each day.
Not only is this Presence responsible for the timing of events as
they occur, but It is responsible for the perfection of the timing.
For example:

A phone call from an old friend when you are feeling sad.

Arriving home at the exact time (although a different time than
you had originally planned) to find that your neighbor is having
an emergency.

Seeing a movie or reading a book that provides insight to a
current life struggle.

The more you become aware of the flow of events in your life,
the easier it will be to recognize the Divine Guidance that is
always readily available to you. It is this Divine Guidance which
can lead you through your life with fewer struggles when you
move through your day with conscious awareness.

Message from the Angel of Mindfulness

To be mindful means to live in the present moment. Your future is created in the present moment and your past becomes healed in the present moment.

To be mindful means to breathe and to be aware of your breath. Your breath connects you to the present moment. Breathe deeply with full awareness. Now, you can powerfully heal your past experiences and create present and future joys.

Message from the
Angel of Trust

When you pray to the Universe, trust that your prayers will be answered as you release your expectations of *how* they will be answered. Then, open your heart to receive your answer.

Message from the Angel of Power

What has power over your life? Is it a relationship, a job or money issues? Actually, it does not matter who or what has power over you. What matters is why. Take a moment to place your hand over your heart and breathe deeply. Then ask yourself why you allow this person or thing to have power over you. (Pay attention to the first answer that you hear!) Next, ask yourself what you need to do to claim your power. As you begin to see the truth that lies behind your choices to give your power away and the limitations you place on getting it back, it is less likely that you will give it away in the future.

Message from the Angel of Vulnerability

Your past experiences in relationships can greatly affect the relationships you have in the present... but only if you allow them. For example, if you have been hurt deeply by a loved one, it may be tempting to close yourself off to being hurt again. Closing off to the hurt, however, not only limits your potential for pain, but also for joy. Allowing yourself to be vulnerable, to risk opening to another . . . to life . . . has far greater rewards. View your past pain as an opportunity for growth, release it and open to the joy in the moment. Remember, you cannot see what is in front of you by looking backwards.

Message from the Angel of Truth

Fear of never being loved unconditionally can be a powerful block to living your life while being true to yourself. Instead of being confident that you are lovable, you deny these very aspects, these wonderful aspects, of yourself in the hope of being loved by another. When you choose to live your life truthfully, your life becomes more than just hanging on or living in survival mode. Being true to who you are means that you show up for life with the intention of full participation, no matter the situation. So the question to ask yourself now is this: "Do you want to continue pretending that you are living or do you want to participate in life. . . all of it?"

Message from the Angel of Belief

Ego is attached to the outcome of all things. Spirit is attached to the effort put into doing anything. If you want to truly believe in yourself, then invest in your spirit and not your ego. Always.

Message from the Angel of Perseverance

When you enter a time of perseverance, do not think of it as a time of struggle. View it as a period of adjustment where your external world is catching up to reflect the incredible soul you are on the inside.

Message from the Angel of Relationships

Be mindful not to lose yourself in your relationships with a partner, friends or family. Your relationships do not define you. The way, however, in which you conduct yourself within them and in all your interactions with others, reflects how you define yourself.

Message from the
Angel of Relationships

True communication arises when you step outside of your
personal attachment to what others share with you and open to
your compassion for their inherent struggles within themselves.

Message from the Angel of Personal Power

Never give away your personal power to others in search for a love that lies within.

Message from the Angel of Emotions

Anger goes against the very nature of who you are. It is a violation of your spirit. To deny your anger, however, is to deny your humanness. Choose to acknowledge your anger, to feel it *and* to release it. Now you can live in cooperation with both aspects of yourself... as a spirit in a human body.

Message from the Angel of Joy

You need to stand in your pain to be able to stand in your joy. This is not to say that one must always precede the other, but rather that the process of feeling precedes both.

Message from the Angel of Spirit

Anxiety results whenever the need to maintain mental control over your life becomes greater than the need to allow Spirit to work through you.

Message from the Angel of Abundance

Commit your life to living spiritually each day by focusing on bringing love into every interaction, including those with yourself. When interacting with others, remove the subconscious question of how their actions and/or choices will affect you and instead ask Spirit how you can best serve It. Now you are moving into authentic abundance.

Message from the
Angel of Attention

Life is a culmination of experiences that are designed to connect
you with the essence of your spirit. To make this connection
requires not only courage, but focused attention on your core life
issues. This focus is fraught with difficulties because of the initial
pain that may be involved as you move through them. The key
piece to remember is that your issues must be addressed eventually and the longer they go un-addressed, the greater the pain.
You have the opportunity to choose to address these issues now
and at the same time, create a nurturing environment in which to
process, release and heal them. Choosing each day to gently focus
on an area or issue in your life breaks them down into a series of
small, manageable hills instead of a large mountain that looms in
front of you. The hills offer you balance while the mountains
offer you peaks and valleys.

So, which do you choose to wear, sneakers or hiking boots?

Message from the Angel of Trust

Trust allows love to flow into your life because it is the basis for bonding with others. When trust is broken, so are the bonds. The initial tendency may be for you to close off to the hurt and pain through withdrawal resulting in closing off your heart to love. All is not lost. You can begin to trust again as you learn to make better choices. For instance, do not place your trust in others. Choose, instead, to place it in yourself and in your ability to make choices that reflect self-love and self-worth. Believe in what your heart tells you. Do not be afraid to see the truth in your situation and to act accordingly. It may not be an easy process in the beginning, but taking the first step will open your life to love. Love is, after all, what your heart truly seeks and all that your spirit knows.

Message from the Angel of Trust

Choosing to trust in yourself and in your ability to make choices that reflect self-love and self-worth is not always an easy path. Trust requires courage and the temporary surrender of security. Courage requires you to listen to your own inner truth while surrendering security means releasing the need for others to validate this truth, your truth. When you need others to validate your choices (your truth) you are clearly saying that you trust them more than you trust yourself. You are giving them your personal power. Instead, remember there are no right or wrong choices, only better ones. Each better choice made with the intention of trusting yourself, deepens your capacity for self-love and self-worth.

Message from the Angel of Release

As the moon goes through its phases of darkness and light, so does your life. Your phases in life may be marked by sorrow and joy or personal growth and integration. But remember, behind each phase is a choice. If you are not happy with your life, then reflect on the choices you have made thus far. Choices made when you are connected to your spirit have the power to create, at all levels of your life, that which your heart deeply seeks. If you are in a phase that requires new choices, believe enough in yourself and in your spirit to have the courage to make them, while releasing what no longer works for you. As you do, you will emerge from the darkness and step into the light... *always*.

Message from the Angel of Nature

When you are feeling tired because of your daily struggles in life, get out into Nature. Nature has a way of healing your soul at a deep level. It is an energy resource that rejuvenates you, allowing you to accomplish all that you desire. Although your life may be too "busy" to want to take this time in such a wonderful healing environment, it is essential for your life. Even five focused minutes a day spent in Nature will dramatically shift your energy levels.

Think about this: Butterflies have to spread their wings in the morning sun because the scales on their wings are actually solar cells. Without this energy resource, they could not fly. You also need to be in tune with your energy resources.

Are you not worth the five minutes?

Message from the Angel of Divine Guidance

Dreams are the essence of life. When you live your dreams, you feel as if you can fly. But sadly enough, many people believe that their wings are broken before they even try to fly. Whether it is a lack of belief in themselves or a lack of support from those closest to them, their dream remains within and left un-lived. However, each person is blessed with gifts and abilities that, although not always unique, can be expressed in unique ways. Your gifts and abilities were designed to help you live out your deepest dreams, and expressing them is your life purpose. Take a close look at what lies within you and give yourself permission to praise, not criticize, what you discover. Then take a deep breath and begin to allow your uniqueness to emerge. Just as a baby bird is awkward when testing its wings, you may also feel unsure and unsteady. But, the baby bird does fly and so can you.

Message from the Angel of Divine Guidance

In life, each individual deeply craves one thing: The need to feel safe and secure. It is this need that is the basis behind every major life choice. These choices often involve money and/or relationships. The illusion behind these choices, however, is that having enough money or being in a loving relationship will provide you with the security you seek. Yet if either of these is lost, so is your feeling of security. Choose, instead, to find a sense of security which can never be taken away from you. Looking to the external world to find it will prove fruitless. You must look within. When you look within, you find and connect with your spirit which, in turn, smoothes your path in the physical world and gives you the security you seek. Your connection with your spirit allows you to begin to sense the invisible presence of the Universe in your life where true security is found.

For it has been said before, when the illusion of the physical world fails to meet your needs, there is only one place to turn and that is within.

Message from the
Angel of Challenge

Life is but a series of experiences designed to lead you more deeply within yourself. This much you know to be true... until these life experiences become challenging and you forget their higher purpose. Did you also know that within you are deeply felt dreams and aspirations that wish to manifest into your life? These dreams and aspirations are also known as your life purpose.

In order to manifest your life purpose you must first go through an initiation process that tests your inner strength, spiritual resources and belief in yourself as a worthy vehicle of positive action. You are being initiated into living your life at a deeper level, a level that requires challenging experiences to test your readiness. They test the strength of your inner foundation, the basis upon which your dreams are built. Awareness of these upcoming experiences can assist you with moving smoothly through them, but it is more important to remember to tap into the inner strength and resources that lie within you.

Message from the Angel of Passion

Passion in your life is absolutely void of meaning if you don't first have a passion for yourself. This passion should be to love yourself fully and completely as you are. People often hold within them fear of self-love. They may believe, for instance, that self-love will result in not needing anyone in their life. Reflect on that for a moment. Does the act of self-love really result in not needing anyone in your life? If that is not your belief, then reflect on what negative belief you hold about self-love that keeps you from actually loving yourself, and then release it.

The truth behind self-love is that as it grows and deepens within you, the capacity of your heart to experience love increases. This is what attracts more people into your life... not the other way around.

Message from the
Angel of Vulnerability

Honest and without pretense... how many people can truly say
that they live this way? When communicating with others, do
you stretch the truth to make yourself sound better or do you not
say anything at all, fearing that you will sound inadequate? At
the same time, there is a part of you that wishes to have or to
deepen a close relationship with someone special. To have close,
intimate relationships, you need to let people see you for who you
really are. If you are unable to open to your vulnerabilities, your
human frailties, you keep people at a distance. The spiritual
strength within your vulnerabilities is that you take the risk in
allowing others to see you are not "perfect". In doing so, you
recognize your own perfection... as you are.

Message from the Angel of Divine Guidance

Many people spend their entire life wishing others would acknowledge them. Throughout your life there has been, and still is, a deeply abiding Presence gently guiding you to the realization that you are loved fully and completely. Since this Presence is not always or easily seen, you may struggle to accept that It is, in fact, present. Yet, when a difficult or challenging issue arises, there is some deeper part of you that instantly calls on this Presence. Instead of trying to validate this Presence (and adding to your struggles), accept It into your life and look for the Divine guidance which is always readily available to lead you towards joy.

Message from the Angel of Purpose

Everyone is born with a life purpose, but not everyone feels they are living it. The confusion sets in when you believe this life purpose should be carried out in the form of a career or a relationship. It is more helpful to view it from a different perspective. For example, your career may be that of a teacher, yet your true life purpose may be to help others learn more about themselves in a loving and supportive environment. Choose nor to let your career or relationship define you or your life. Instead, decide how you can live your life purposefully. Then, the tangible means of living your life purpose will begin to manifest and you will truly be living your life.

Message from the Angel of Attention

Lost relationships; lack of financial means; ill health; and an unfulfilling career . . . are some or all of these issues a main focus in your life? Remember, your life is only a reflection of where you choose to focus your attention. You can either focus on the challenges in your life or on the deeper experiences brought to you by them. For instance, you may have lost a relationship either through a parting of the ways or through death. The issue is loss, but the experience is one of love, most likely self-love, meaning you now have an opportunity to find self-love regardless of who is in your life.

Choosing to focus on the experience of your struggles allows you to move through them with less pain since you can now view them as vehicles for self-discovery.

Message from the Angel of Challenge

Challenges are in your life so that you may recognize your own value and self-worth, but you must believe in yourself first so that you can rise up to meet them and to move through them. Your self belief will lead others to believing in you . . . not the other way around. This is how you find your self-worth. Once it is found, no one will ever be able to take it away from you.

Message from the
Angel of Passion

Actions taken in anger do not transform but only build stronger
defenses. Actions arising from passion, anger that has been
transformed, inspire and motivate a sense of unity among all. It is
in this unity that true, lasting changes arise. Seek then to
transform your anger into passion rather than turn your anger
into action.

Message from the Angel of Light

It is only when there has been darkness that one appreciates light and it is only light which dispels darkness. The amount of light you invite into your life foretells what your life experiences will be.

Message from the Angel of Divine Guidance

Answers to our greatest struggles are always present within. Whether we choose to recognize them, however, is a conscious choice we need to make even when the darkest of hours are upon us.

Message from the Angel of Possibilities

Illusion: You *know* you have limitations.

Truth: You believe you have limitations until you choose to *know* that anything and everything is possible when you are connected to the power of your spirit.

This message is dedicated to the physically challenged women skiers who participated in the 2000 Chevy Truck Downhill Alpine Championship for the Disabled. Your spirits are an incredible source of inspiration to us all.

Message from the Angel of Dreams

When the effort to keep your dreams alive seems too great, ask yourself this one question: "Are your dreams nurtured within the space of your soul or within the confines of your ego?"

Dreams of the ego are tiring because you view them as a source of validation and self-worth. Loss of the dream results in the loss of your self-worth. Any feelings of fulfillment from these dreams are fleeting since they are filled with unreasonable expectations versus authentic expression.

Dreams from your soul space are the essence of life. These dreams have passion and create the deepest feelings of fulfillment. When you are connected to your soul, not only is the manifestation of your dreams effortless, it's magical.

So which do you choose, fleeting fulfillment or everlasting passion and magic?

Message from the Angel of Commitment

The freedom that is found in making a commitment only arises when one understands her reason for choosing to make the commitment… and fear cannot be a reason. When you understand this message deeply, the door will be opened for miracles to flow to you.

Message from the Angel of Belief

Have you ever noticed that your tendency to doubt your gifts and abilities is greater than your tendency to believe in them? Have you ever realized that you say you cannot do something more than you say you can? These doubts make little sense, especially when you know deep within your heart you can do it, that you are, in fact, greatness itself. The moment you commit yourself to thinking this way will be the moment you begin to live your greatness.

So please, let us stop the self-doubt, shall we? After all, you have been down this road before and you know that it is not where you really want to be. Today, take the road of self-confidence. You will find it to be a wonderful ride!

Message from the Angel of Purpose

If you fear what you will create in your life by choosing to follow your life path, remember the fear does not compare to the sorrow you will experience if you choose not to walk it.

Message from the Angel of Life

Lovingly the angel spoke, "Now remember, your experiences are not who you are, you are never alone and, not only are you completely lovable but you are Love itself." Taking the little soul by the hand and giving her a big hug the angel continued, "Until we meet again."

Excitedly the little soul made her way towards Earth. Her life journey had now begun and her fellow soul mates awaited her arrival.

Message from the Angel of Love

From the diary of a human . . .

Silence.

Emptiness.

Something is missing, but I am not quite sure what it is. And then realization dawns. . . it's my heart that is missing. It seems that I gave it to you for safekeeping. But when you left, you took my heart with you. Why did I trust you with such a special part of me? Why did I even give you a part of myself to begin with? The pain is so great and the loss... unbearable. But really, the pain is not due to the loss of you, but for the loss of me.

Now, I know that . . .

Giving you a part of me was not love.

Trusting you with my heart over trusting me with it was also not love.

Love is sharing the self not giving the self away.

The lesson learned . . .

When you give you lose, but when you share, you always win. Only then will you be able to love like you have never been hurt before. For when you share love, you share yourself, and your heart swells with joy. But unless you hold onto your heart you will never know this joy.

Message from the
Angel of Soul Love

There is nothing romantic about love when one person sacrifices who he or she is for the love of another. True love only manifests when each person is free to be all that they can be and more. Your soul cannot, and will not, settle for anything less than its fullest expression. Make this the love that you truly seek and your destiny will be the incredible experience of your soul's eternal love.

Message from the Angel of Manifestation

During the process of manifesting your deepest dreams, you may encounter times when confusion reigns supreme. Usually this state of confusion is fleeting in nature, but if it begins to feel like a close, personal friend then you have reached a critical point in your life, a point of surrender.

Surrender does not mean that you let go of your dreams. Surrender means you release how you think they *should* come to you. This means you turn over the details of manifesting your dreams to a higher part of your Self. Not only does this higher Self create from a place of Love, but your happiness is Its number one priority.

In the meantime, your role is to hold onto the vision for your life, to hold onto your dreams. Trust your *Self* for your dreams are coming to you.

Message from the Angel of Acceptance

Prejudice.
Hate.
Racism.
Discrimination.

Pick whichever word you prefer, but know one thing. World peace cannot begin until there is self-acceptance. Self-acceptance precedes the acceptance of others and it begins the moment we acknowledge our inner beauty and uniqueness while releasing self-hate and self-discrimination. The fact is, there truly is no room in our lives for anything but self-acceptance or self-love. As a matter of fact, without them, our lives become an incredible waste of time.

It is the beginning of a brave, new world . . .

Message from the Angel of Love

Gently but surely you feel it. Something seems different within you and yet, there is a feeling of familiarity . . . like a long lost friend. A subtle fear arises as you recall past memories and the pain that comes with them. It cannot be, you think to yourself. But there is no denying it, for the time has come. Love has entered your life.

A ripple of excitement moves through your heart as you move into full awareness of its presence and it speaks to you . . . "The time has come for me to live my purpose, to carry out my destiny. I have been closed for too long to the love that swells within these walls. I long to share it with you . . . with a partner . . . with friends . . . with all who cross my path."

"Do nor fear this love," your heart urges, "for this time, I will not love to receive love. Nor will I love because I fear I am nor lovable. Instead, I will love because it is who I am and I wish to share who I am with the world."

You agree, knowing deeply that a heart which does not love dies a slow death with each beat.

Message from the
Angel of Expression

One day the master asked his student, "Little one, why do you look so sad?"

To which his student replied, "I feel paralyzed by life because I have no understanding of where I am headed. I have created a life vision, but I am struggling to believe that I can live it. I am afraid to believe in myself and in my vision. It seems so much easier not to dream, to stay with what appears safe and familiar."

"Each morning when I awake, my whole future stretches before me like an empty canvas. I hold the paintbrush in my hand with a vision of what I want to paint, but then I fear making the first brush stroke. Question after question runs through my thoughts . . . What if I start painting at the wrong place? What if halfway through the painting I dont like the colors I have chosen to express? What if I paint a perfect picture and then have no other creative inspirations? Or what if I paint an incredible picture that I enjoy for years to come? What will that mean for me?"

The master looked lovingly at his student and replied, "Well, you can continue to choose to ponder your doubts and questions over and over again while never experiencing your answer, but one fact will always remain: There is an empty canvas before you and in the grand scheme of life 'what if' questions become a poor excuse for living."

Message from the Angel of Meaning

You have a personal destiny that seeks expression in this lifetime. To discover and live this destiny requires that you look within and identify where you wish to bring meaning into your life. The greatest misconception is that life brings meaning to you. The greatest truth is that you bring meaning to life.

Now, how do you choose to live today?

Message from the Angel of Freedom

Freedom comes to you the moment you see yourself at the center of all your experiences. This means that if you want to experience:

Love: Love yourself first.
Financial abundance: Recognize your own inherent value.
Fulfillment: Evaluate how you fulfill your own needs.
Spiritual well-being: Reflect on your level of commitment to a daily spiritual practice.
Health: Make each choice serve your highest good.

This is the way to freedom.

Message from the Angel of Vulnerability

Do you sometimes feel lost wondering what life is really all about? Do you sometimes feel alone as you walk along your path in this world? Do you sometimes question if you even have a path to follow? Do you sometimes wish for a sign that will let you know how your life will turn out?

When you find yourself alone in your deepest moments of vulnerability, do not close the door on the Sacred in your life, invite the Sacred in. Your vulnerability will be transformed into the greatest miracle you have ever lived and you will know deeply:

Life does have meaning and purpose.
You are never, ever alone.
You do have a path to follow and it is waiting for you.
Your sign is your life and the Sacred is your life force. Wherever one is, the other will also be.

Message from the Angel of Passion

One day while eating lunch with a friend, he shared with me his stories about his trip to a third world country. These stories included his observations of the tremendous poverty, overwhelming disease, environmental pollution and seemingly unending discrimination of the people. As he continued to talk, tears came to my eyes and a deep sadness filled my heart. When he finished, I asked him if he felt inspired to do something to help the people in this country. Sadly, he said no. He did not think that one person could really make a difference. Thus, this Angel message:

The next time you encounter an individual or global situation that brings you sadness, frustration or inspiration, do not turn away from it. Turn towards it and open yourself to the passion that is rising within your heart. To deny your ability to help another or to deny that you alone can make a difference in this world is to ultimately deny your purpose for existence. After all, you are not only Spirit's eyes and hands, you are Spirit's heart. Both your passion and your love are needed today in this world.

Message from the Angel of Life Purpose

When you receive an inspiration or a calling to make a difference in the world, why do you question your ability to do it? Why do you question who you are to do this or that? When Spirit moves you, why do you not automatically reply "No problem, consider it done!"?

Life is not an interview to see whether or not you are capable for the job at hand, nor is it a test to see whether or not you have gifts to share. You have already been interviewed and you have already been hired! Your responsibility is to live out your life purpose without hesitation!

Got it? Good. Now, get busy. The world awaits your contribution!

147

Message from the Angel of Love

You ask for love to enter your life . . . and then you push it away when a partner arrives.

You ask for love to enter your life . . . and then settle for less than what you heart desires.

You ask for love to enter your life . . . and you don't believe that you can truly have a loving partnership.

So now love asks you, "What does it take for you to believe you are lovable?"

Love is at your door right now. You only have to open it to let love in.

Message from the Angel of Inspiration

Imagine one day you are visited by an Angel who shares the following guidance with you:

"Little one, I know there have been times when you have felt both frustrated and confused about your life. I understand that you have wondered many times about what it is that you are supposed to do with it. I am here today to share the insight that this lifetime is only a dress rehearsal for 'The Real Thing'."

" In this lifetime, you are not only the actor, but you are also the writer, director and producer of your play. All the necessary characters are in your life to help make your production a huge success. Since this is an incredible opportunity to practice living before the curtain rises, have fun exploring and experimenting with any and all ideas that come to you. Release your fears and trust deeply that it will turn out perfectly in the end. Today like every day, the stage is yours!"

Message from the Angel of Seasons

Once upon a time, the seeds were planted. Then they were watered, nurtured and exposed to various natural elements as the gardener waited patiently to view the seeds' blossoms. Slowly, but with purpose, the seeds pushed past their shells and began to grow, reaching tentatively for the sun, for the light. Days passed . . . more sun . . . more nurturing and buds began developing. Their support was now firmly rooted. More days passed as the gardener excitedly awaited the blossoms. Then quietly and without fanfare, the day arrived. Gently and gracefully the blossoms opened to the full expression of their beauty as the gardener opened to receive the incredible miracle before him. But when he looked closer, he noticed that one of the buds had not blossomed. He shook his head sadly. Even though surrounded by the blossoming beauty of all the other flowers, the one bud had remained tightly closed. For you see, this flower did not believe in itself. It did not have the courage to risk opening to its beauty so it may be shared with the entire world.

The gardener turned to walk away pondering the unopened bud. Maybe next season, he thought to himself.

Will this be your season to blossom? Do you dare show the world your beauty? It is entirely your choice.

Message from the Angel of Memories

Ah, the sweet seduction of memories . . . calling you back to a time long past. They beckon. They tease. They can be merciless in their hold on you and the temptation to stay with them, powerful. If you find you are living your life more through your past memories than your present experiences, do not believe for a minute they are your friend. Resist with all your might to give in to them for their fulfillment will be brief. Lingering memories only fill you with an energy of a past which no longer exists, while present opportunities of wonder are missed. Instead, be grateful for your memories and gently release them, bringing your attention fully to the present moment. Now, the belief in yourself enhances your ability to create new experiences that can, and will, surpass the old memories. You are opening a door through which the magic of life can now flow.

Message from the Angel of Joy

Joy comes to you the moment you can celebrate another person's success without comparison. You have a path to walk in this lifetime that is uniquely yours. Any time spent looking at what someone else is doing with their life is wasted energy, unless, of course, you are celebrating their successes with them. Your success gives others permission to be successful and vice-versa, although it is easy to forget the vice-versa part. Thus celebrating another person's success is also a celebration of your own success. Remember this little tidbit too: Success is not measured by who or what you have in your life. Success is having the courage to express who you are from the depths of your soul; to dream abundantly; and, to believe in your dreams while having the courage to follow them.

Message from the Angel of Vision

A vision for your life begins and ends with you. It also requires that you take the first step. Now the question becomes this: "Do you have the courage to take that step?"

Message from the Angel of Tenderness

When you are self-critical, it is a like walking on a long road to nowhere. Self-critical thoughts and words only sap your energy and the energy of those you interact with on a daily basis. Tenderness towards you, however, is a completely different story. Not only does it allow you to make healthy changes in all areas of your life, it places you in a state of expansion which attracts abundance to all levels of your life. The next time you feel inclined to be harsh with yourself, take a deep breath and try a little tenderness instead. You have absolutely nothing to lose and so much to gain!

Message from the
Angel of Personal Power

Life is about relationships, relationships with yourself and with others. Life is also about love, the love we have for Self and for others. When you sacrifice and compromise the Self in order to be in a relationship you give away your personal power. Thus, the relationship will eventually end. Your spirit never allows you to compromise your*Self* for long. It knows that you are more than that. So embrace who you are, claim your personal power and let it shine for all to see. As you do this, your relationships will move to higher levels of interaction where the love experienced will be incredible!

Message from the
Angel of Inner Authority

One day I asked Spirit, "How do I get to know you?"

To which a Voice replied, "As you know yourself, you know Me."

"How do I do that?" I asked.

The Voice then replied, "Pay attention to your feelings in any given situation. They are your roadmap to yourself . . . to your inner authority . . . to your spirit."

"Well," I replied, "to be honest, I am not sure of my feelings concerning anything."

"Then," the Voice said, "it appears that you have some work to do."

Message from the
Angel of Sustenance

Webster defines the word sustenance as *supplying or being supplied with the necessities of life.* . This type of sustenance can be seen in the living of your day to day as you meet both your physical and emotional needs. Webster also defines sustenance as *something that gives support, endurance or strength*. This part of the definition indicates a need in your life which is spiritual in nature. Spiritual needs can be met through a daily spiritual practice. A daily spiritual practice, however, is not a luxury. It is a choice that needs to be made over and over again. It is what nourishes and sustains you when the physical world fails to do so. After all, you do consist of a body, a mind and a spirit. Isn't it time you began giving the world behind your eyes the same attention you give the world before your eyes?

Message from the
Angel of Expansiveness

If you are experiencing struggle in any of your relationships, then ask yourself which you prefer: conclusions or solutions? Conclusions in relationships often create limitations and struggle since they leave little room for personal growth or change. Although the human tendency is to draw conclusions, you can move to a more expanded perspective. Doing so will allow solutions to your relational challenges to become known, thus deepening the capacity to create more love in your life. In reality all relationships are organic, meaning that they are always growing and changing. Embracing growth instead of resisting it will go a long way towards reducing struggle.

So the question again is this: Which do you prefer, conclusions or solutions?

Message from the Angel of Freedom

Believing that your external environment needs to change before you can feel happy or free from anxiety keeps you a prisoner of your own life. True freedom arises when you focus within and embrace the power of your spirit. It is only your spirit that can transcend crisis when your mind is reeling with bewilderment and panic. This connection with your spirit *is* the key to your freedom.

Message from the Angel of Freedom

The silent witness of your life is your spirit. When your ego wants to project into and live in the future, causing you to worry or to fear loss, come back to your spirit. To do this, you need to pay attention to your thoughts, pulling them back to the present moment. This practice may not be easy initially, but with consistent effort you will find the freedom you seek. The surprise occurs when you realize you have carried this freedom with you at all times!

Message from the Angel of Acceptance

"Good" and "bad" experiences do not exist. Only experiences exist. It is your ego that labels experiences as either "good" or "bad" because its identity is tied to them. Your spirit knows that you are incredibly special. To feel any different about yourself based on your experiences means you are not connected to your spirit. Thus, these experiences have shown you who you are not.

Once you truly accept your spirit's truth, all your choices, including what you believe about yourself, will be aligned with this truth and so, then, will your experiences.

Message from the Angel of Health

During the course of your life, there will be days in which health will elude you. When this occurs, recognize that you are learning a powerful lesson, a lesson in gratitude. Often it is only through the loss of health that you become grateful for it. If you are healthy now, then celebrate it by nurturing and caring for yourself regularly. If you are currently experiencing health challenges, then be grateful for the areas of your body that are healthy while loving and nurturing those that are not. Above all, live in gratitude for your life while always bringing the best of who you are to it. It is just this perspective of gratitude that will create and sustain your health. Always!

Message from the
Angel of Past, Present & Future

If your belief of yourself is based on your past experiences or the potential fulfillment of future experiences, then you will create struggle in your life. All that you are is found only in the present moment, for this is where awareness to your deeper Self is accessed and lived. Reflecting back on your past experiences and then releasing them as your source of personal identification is extremely powerful and necessary. Keeping an empowered vision for your life is also part of living your creativity, as long as you do nor lose your sense of Self. Do you see the power of living in the present moment? Your past is healed and your future is created in the present moment. There is nothing else than the present moment. When you accept this fact, all struggles can finally be released.

Message from the Angel of Healing

The belief that you need to heal is false. You do not need to heal. You are healed. You are perfection in and of itself. Life is a process of remembering that you are healed and perfect, even if your personal experiences may suggest otherwise. The fear of remembering this is only because you fear that loking deep within will result in seeing imperfections and failures. Feelings of imperfection and failure are only the result of not trusting your innermost truth. When you live in fear of your authentic Self, you will experience struggle in the form of failure . . . always wishing you did things differently. If you align your life in acknowledgment of your own truth, there will only be perfec-tion. The process of remembering can sometimes be painful as you push through false beliefs, but there is a pot of gold awaiting your discovery. For you see, this pot of gold is you, the authentic you, grounded in sweet perfection.

Message from the Angel of Personal Growth

As you progress through life, the process of self-awareness often brings struggle. You may experience deep personal growth followed by happiness, only to find yourself struggling all over again. Understanding that you can learn from your struggles is important, but there are times when you may reach a point when you feel like you are constantly struggling. You may wish to have life flow more smoothly. It will. Life becomes easier as you progress through personal challenges. Pain may arise initially, though, because they have acted as a block to your personal growth for so long.

Be patient with yourself and recognize that challenges with struggle go in cycles, much as relationships. First there is excitement, and then there is challenge . . . the uncovering . . . the process of discovery. There is a time to rest and a time to question. Each time this process leads you deeper within. As you move deeper within, your struggles lessen due to greater self awareness. You begin to understand the higher spiritual purpose in every interaction and experience, the higher purpose being that of personal growth. Continue confidently on your life journey, remembering that growth is the key to a life filled with abundance and joy.

Message from the
Angel of Willingness

Do you feel your personality is aware of the wisdom which lies within your soul? Unfortunately, the answer is most likely "no." Yet you have a tool with which to get to know yourself better, a tool that allows you to connect with what your soul already knows about you as a person. This tool comes in the form of relationships. Other people are in your life to help you deepen yourself as a person. In order to maximize growth, you must be willing to release preconceived notions. Each day is a new day and when truly viewed that way it allows you to see the world with "fresh eyes." This, in turn, encourages you to see the growing potential in others which reflects the growing potential within you.

Message from the Angel of Divine Guidance

Divine guidance is readily available to you in every moment. In order to better experience Divine guidance, you need to begin to see the inter-connectedness of all things. For example, does it seem that you have struggled to feel loved or to feel validated as a result of your past life experiences? Your experiences were not a means of punishment from an unloving Universe; rather it was at these times that the Universe held you closely so that you could use these experiences to find self-love and self-worth. The major themes your life has revolved around are the areas which your soul has chosen to deepen itself more fully in this lifetime. Begin now to see the bigger picture of your life experiences, not as a life filled with pain and suffering, but as a means to accept love and joy into your life while helping others to find it also.

Message from the Angel of Tenderness

Tenderness is a profound spiritual quality which has a far-reaching and powerful impact on the world. In order for tenderness to be used effectively it must first be used on a smaller scale . . . starting with yourself. You cannot share kind words with others until you share kind words with yourself. The challenge that lies before you is to begin to recognize the tone of your inner dialogue. Are your words self-loving and self-validating or are they harsh and self-critical? Only tender-loving words have the power to create lasting positive change. Choose now to use them generously with yourself and others.

Message from the Angel of Vulnerability

Repeat patterns . . . repeat patterns . . . and more repeat patterns. Does this sound like your life? Do you want to break these patterns because you are tired and frustrated? Do you believe there is more to life, that there is more to you? Then make the choice to open yourself to your own vulnerabilities. Take stock of your life, noting where you pretend to be someone other than yourself. Instead of saying you do not need love in your life, reflect on the thought that you may be afraid to have love in your life or you fear you are unlovable. This is not a sign of weakness, but rather a sign indicating an opportunity for deeper growth.

Closing yourself off to love or any other emotion which is frightening or risks hurt and pain keeps you living in an illusion and prevents you from experiencing life at a deeper, richer level.

Message from the Angel of Courage

As you journey on your path through life with all its struggles and joys, take a moment to look around. Are you living life to the fullest with enthusiastic participation or are you watching life pass you by?

As you reflect on your life, note the role fear plays. Fear acts as block to taking risks and stepping outside your comfort zone. Summon courage to push through fears, to expand your world and horizons. Feel the thrill of taking a chance on something that has no known outcome and open yourself to the dramatic impact this can have on your life. In addition, through your actions, you will inspire others to do the same, to toss caution to the winds . . . to really live life now.

Message from the Angel of Love

Love is real.

Love is all that exists.

All else is an illusion.

Seek to find love and you will always be searching. Choose to experience Love and It will find you.

Message from the Angel of Connection

Many people want to believe that the world before their eyes is all that exists and is real. Your life purpose is to remember your spiritual nature, the world which exists behind your eyes, and to build the bridge between the physical and spiritual worlds. Your strong bridge inspires others to build strong bridges. This is your destiny.

Message from the
Angel of Family

Remember this . . . Your family experiences are present to remind
you:

To embrace your creativity and individuality. To release any fears
of failure expecting only success. To believe in yourself and in
your value always.

Above all, remember that this is *your* life journey. Only you can
walk it.

Message from the Angel of Expression

What you believe to be true about yourself, will be true. What you believe to be true about others will also be true. In order to create a space of authentic expression for yourself and others, you must choose to hold the highest vision of every person, including yourself. To hold this highest vision of you and others means to perceive them coming from their soul space in all situations. This perception will thus create that very experience . . . and it will be powerful.

Message from the Angel of Love

Although people may sometimes get lost in their lives and forget to tell you they love you . . .

Although people may not believe they are lovable and may not be able to tell you they love you . . .

Although some people may need to hear they are lovable before they can tell you they love you . . .

Never forget that you are lovable. Tell yourself this each day. This way, your self-love will be a gentle reminder for others to love themselves too.

Message from the Angel of Nature

Nature, like life itself, is an unending cycle. The seed becomes the flower only to rejoin with Mother Earth once again. You are like the seed which means there will be times to withdraw from life to nurture yourself. You are also like the flower and it will be your inner light that encourages your fullest blossoming. You and Mother Earth will also be rejoined so you may return to blossom once again.

Embrace the cycles of your life with gentleness and understanding and you will find much joy.

Message from the Angel of Perception

Alone.
Lonely.
Solitude.

All of the above words have similar and yet, different meanings. Basically though, it is just the perception of the situation which changes.

Message from the Angel of Past Lives

Another world, some other time . . .
we believed that our love would always endure.
But our promises of love were broken the day when
Fate stepped in as our love turned to loss and pain.

Another world, some other time . . .
although we look different now and
our life roles have changed,
it is our essence, our love, which still
remains the same.

Another world, some other time . . .
with our lessons learned and
love both found and lost,
there is one thing we know,
of which we can be sure.
Wherever we are,
no matter how far,
should Fate step in to pull us apart,
we know that the words will never
be, "Good-bye,"
but only, "Until we meet again."

For 'Squirt'

178

Message from the Angel of Soul Love

I turn away from You.
I do not know who You are.
You are a Stranger and I fear You.
And yet, there is something . . .
I want to know You.
I want to believe in You.
But here . . . I am safe.
You touch me.
Your hand covers my heart.
You whisper, "Let Me in."
My eyes open and I see them now,
the lines in the sand.
You take my hand in Your hand and
together we brush them away,
Now, my heart opens and Love walks in.
You whisper again, "Boundaries on Love
are like lines in the sand, they are not
permanent. All it takes is a choice to know
Me, to open your heart to Me."

Message from the Angel of Dreams

When you arrive at a time in life and you do not know: how to make your life work; where else to turn; or when you want to give up on yourself or on your dreams, recognize that you need to surrender to your soul. It is in the surrendering that the space opens for dreams without limits to manifest.

Now, the magic can begin . . .

Message from the Angel of Soul-lutions

There will be times when life is easy and times when life is more difficult. But always, answers to your life questions lie within. You must only turn within to hear them. Turn within to that place deep inside and listen. Listen to the voice of your soul. Your soul always remembers who you are . . . and who you can be.

Message from the
Angel of Guidance

Each day and each minute you are receiving guidance for your life and life questions. Unfortunately, though, you often greet your guidance with resistance or disbelief while knowing deep within your heart what you must do. So the next time you are tempted to ask your guidance what you should do or why something is happening to you, ask yourself this: Why do you fear acting on what you know in your heart to be true? At least now you will be moving in a forward direction.

Message from the Angel of Truth

No one can tell you the truth about who you are. You, however, can know the truth of who you are and share it with others. It is through expressing your truth that you assist others with acknowledging their own truth about themselves.

Message from the
Angel of Value

The woman said to Spirit, "I recognize the value I bring to my relationships. I am humorous, insightful, compassionate and positive. But, when I am alone, I struggle to recognize my value. So I feel that my value is only reflected when I am with others."

The man said to Spirit, "I recognize the value I bring to my relationships. I am fun, supportive, understanding and encouraging. But, when I am alone, I struggle to recognize my value. So I feel that my value is only reflected when I am with others."

And Spirit replied to both, "Then you need to develop a relationship with your Self. In this relationship, embody all the qualities you have within when you are with others and cultivate new ones. Only then will you be able to recognize your value when you are alone, and then you will not feel alone."

Message from the Angel of Divine

To be Divine means to embrace your potential and to live it. To embrace the Divine within means to embrace the Truth that all is possible. If you should ever find yourself believing in limitations, remember that this is not who you are and re-connect with your spirit again. Your spirit is the pathway to the Divine.
It is All That Is.

Message from the Angel of Glory

When you desire to see how glorious you truly are, remember this: Your glory cannot be seen, with your eyes. It can only be felt with your heart.

Message from the Angel of Release

If not for struggle, one would not know herself. But, it is a wise person that embraces herself first, thus releasing the need for struggle at all.

Message from the
Angel of Possibilities

What you believe to be impossible becomes just that, impossible. What you believe to be possible opens the door to limitless opportunities. But first you must believe.

Message from the Angel of Spirit

Each day is a new day and each day brings with it new opportunities to deepen your life journey. Wise is the person who allows her spirit to lead her on this journey, for only then will she find the love and joy she seeks.

Where is your spirit leading you today?

Message from the Angel of Personal Growth

You are and you are always becoming. Who you choose to be is your choice. Who you choose to be is reflected not only in your thoughts, but, in your words and actions. Choose from your heart and who you choose to be will be wonderful.

Message from the Angel of Spirit

Never question your gifts or abilities but always question whether you are connected to your ego or your spirit when using them.

Message from the Angel of Attitude

It is not the quality of life that counts, but the quality of your attitude with which you greet life that makes all the difference.

Message from the
Angel of Life

When a person is unloving to another, it means she forgot to love herself.

When a person judges another, it means she forgot to accept herself.

When a person discourages another, it means she forgot to believe in herself and in her potential.

Remember this . . .
When you want love, love yourself first. When you want acceptance, accept yourself first. And when you want to live your dreams, believe in yourself first . . . always.

Message from the
Angel of Creativity

Each day, no matter how it is lived, becomes a new page in your life story. Each day you have a new opportunity to lead the story in a different direction with new characters, new opportunities, new challenges and fresh perspectives. Your story can either be a bestseller or a total bomb. But the best part is it is entirely up to you!

Message from the Angel of Commitment

When you create a vision for your life and focus your energy towards it, you attract everything needed for its fulfillment.

Message from the
Angel of Inner Strength

Many times during the course of our lives we pray for pains or difficulties to be taken away. Yet we can choose to perceive challenges as opportunities to develop inner strength and compassion. Through this choice, we open ourselves to experience the transformation of challenges into incredible gifts of personal growth.

Today gratefully embrace challenges with the full understanding that they are only a temporary situation leading you into a deeper experience of yourself.

Message from the Angel of Time

Slowly, the sun sets as the sky fills with a warm glow. Yet another day is ending. Another day lived well, another day loved well. Or maybe not, as you tell yourself there is always tomorrow. But how many times will you continue to put off living and loving until tomorrow? Today, bring tomorrow's promise into the present moment. After all, today is all you have been promised.

Message from the Angel of Destiny

From the shadows you crawl.
Towards the light you move.
It is time for you to shine.
Destiny beckons . . . and you must follow. You can no longer be a
stranger to yourself.

Message from the Angel of Competition

The Ego vs. The Soul

The Ego views competition as an event where someone either wins or loses and this becomes a form of self-validation or loss of self worth.

The Soul embraces competition as an opportunity to bring the best of who it is to each situation while inspiring others to do the same.

Message from the Angel of Abundance

The question of receiving abundance into your life is never about self-worth. Do not ask yourself, "Am I worthy to receive?" Instead, ask yourself, "Am I willing to receive?"

You are a miracle and the abundance in your life is a reflection of your willingness to acknowledge the Divine within. Through sharing your abundance with others, you acknowledge the Divine within them.

Message from the Angel of Dreams

Life is but a dream and without dreams, life ceases to exist. Thus, always dream and always live your dreams for it is the greatest gift you can ever give yourself and others. Living your dreams not only gives you life, but it inspires others to live more fully, since dreams are a reflection of your essence. This fullest expression of yourself, of your dreams, is your only acceptable life path.

Message from the
Angel of Potential

Potential.
From a spark to a form.
Many lifetimes, many journeys.
But this time . . .
you know who you are.
This time you remember
you are potential made manifest.

Message from the Angel of Passion

You cannot go back and undo something. You can only go forward. How you live your life now, in this moment, is all that matters. Do not live the moment by trying to make up for the past. Choose to live today with integrity and love, fully committed to your spiritual nature. Living this way is living with passion and truth, your truth. Be who you came here to be.

Message from the
Angel of Life Force

Breath, the essence of life, not only nourishes your body but your mind and spirit too. Take a moment to connect with your breath. Is it shallow and uneven? Are you just going through the motions? If so, rest assured that this is also how you are moving through life, going through the motions of living.

Begin now to deepen your breathing consciously making your in-breath equal to your out-breath. This presence with your life force not only aligns your body, mind and spirit, but your life becomes all about living.

Message from the Angel of Life Purpose

You say you wish for a life map so you can know where to go, which way to turn and when to rest. You believe that having this map will resolve your struggles and finally you will know your purpose; you will know where you are headed in life. Trust me, my friend, when I tell you a map is not what you seek. What you seek is a connection to your Spirit which knows no limitations.

To make this connection, take a journey out to any natural environment while the sun sets, filling the sky with its glorious colors. For it is here that Love steals into the stillness of your heart as the expansiveness of your surroundings fills you with awe. It is here realization dawns that your journey though life is a map-less one and is guided by a Higher Force. Your purpose is to invite this Force into your life so that it may lead you to know yourself, to know Love and to live your purpose.

Message from the Angel of Trust

Trust starts with you. Value your thoughts, intuitions, instincts and feelings, for they are the voice of inner guidance. When you trust your inner guidance above all else, you will discover a very important Truth in life: When you trust yourself first, you are then able to trust others.

Message from the Angel of Love

How to *know* Love:

Choose it. Choose it again. Choose it until you arrive at the point which is choice-less and you *know* Love.

Message from the
Angel of Inspiration

People come and people go in your life. Only certain people enter your life touching it in a way that forever alters you. Through their love, inner strength, encouragement and dedication, they inspire you to be all that you can be and more. They may come in the form of friends, family teachers or mentors. Whatever their role, they can only show you the doorway to your potential. You, however, must choose to walk through it. In our final hour, our celebration of life will not be how well we have lived, but rather, how well we have loved and how we have opened our hearts to receive love.

This Angel Message is dedicated to my mom. Your life has been a living testimony to love. Thank you, for showing me the doorway to my potential. I love you, always.

Message from the Angel of Stewardship

In honor of Earth Day and dedicated to the wonderful dolphins playing today in the Santa Monica Bay. Thank you for the incredible gift and for the gentle reminder that we are not owners, but rather stewards of this planet.

You are the mirror, we are the reflection.
We are the mirror, you are the reflection.

Spinning high into the air, riding the ocean's waves, watching you, our hearts fill with joy as we stand on the beach and smile. Through your playfulness we connect again with our childlike wonder and awe. Your presence serves to remind us of life's magic, a magic that would all too quickly disappear without our love and concern. Watching you we realize that what we take away from you, we also take away from ourselves.

You are the mirror, we are the reflection.
We are the mirror, you are the reflection.

Message from the Angel of Health

"Release your fears," It says.
You do not listen.
"Love me," It says.
You close your heart.
"Nourish me," It says.
You turn away.

Now the tears of sadness fall as your body breaks down and health fades. In a much softer voice, your body speaks once again, "I only want you to release the fears you hold within. I only seek to be loved and nourished. Please do not be afraid of me. I am your friend. I only wish to serve you but I cannot do so if you do not allow me. Know that I love you, always, even if you cannot return it."

Message from the Angel of Choice

Choose to see the beauty in others and you will know your own beauty. Choose to judge others and your destiny will be that of self-judgment. Herein lies the gift of choice.

.

Message from the
Angel of Willpower

Will-power does not mean pushing ahead when you encounter
resistance. Nor does it mean giving up when obstacles are met.
Will-power means focused attention and attunement to your
spirit, your spirit which always has your dreams and desires as its
priority.

Message from the
Angel of Inner Strength

The achievement of your goals only serves to confirm your inner strength while it is the process of attaining your goals that develops it.

Message from the Angel of Destiny

To be called to live one's destiny is one thing, but to live it . . . another.

Message from the
Angel of Loyalty

Loyalty, to the extent that it betrays one's moral values, should not be called loyalty, but stupidity.

Message from the
Angel of Leadership

The call of leadership is the greatest call one could ever answer.
Each day you are called to be a leader through your thoughts,
words and actions. Your goal: To create other leaders through
inspiration.

Message from the Angel of Safety

After wearing a mask for so long, it is normal not to feel safe without it. In your safety, however, do you wear the mask or does it wear you?

Message from the Angel of Awareness

Cultivate awareness so that it is brought into every moment of your living. Awareness brought into each moment means moments no longer exist. Then there is only life.

Message from the Angel of Experiences

Words cannot explain experiences fully, only the meaning *behind* the experiences.

Message from the Angel of Integration

The body, mind and spirit diet:

Food fuels the body, thinking fuels the mind and Love fuels the spirit.

Message from the Angel of Expression

There are no "supposed to's" or "should's" in life. Life is about being clear with what you want to do and making the choices which will take you there.

Message from the
Angel of Love

When one opens her heart to receive Love, Love enters. This is
your calling in life and there is no greater calling. Do you choose
to answer this call?

Message from the Angel of Attitude

You have embarked on a journey from which you cannot turn back. The attitude with which you walk your journey however, is your choice.

Message from the Angel of Creation

When you create for your highest good and the highest good of all, your entire creation and manifestation process will be effortless.

Message from the Angel of Meditation

When one brings awareness into her daily life, one moves into a level of consciousness that becomes All That Is. When one attempts to live life through knowledge and understanding, All That Is remains hidden. You cannot think about something and at the same time experience it. To think about your experience at the time you experience it leads to separation and you move away from what is the here and now into identification of one's self with the experience. Meditation occurs when one is in the here and now regardless of what you are doing.

Message from the Angel of Partnership

Are you participating in a partnership with another person to feel loved or are you sharing love with another person that is reflective of your self-love? One of these choices leads to disappointment while the other leads to fulfillment.

Message from the Angel of Vision

What you believe about yourself to be true, will be true. Thus, always hold the highest vision of yourself.

Message from the Angel of Living

Steps to a powerful life:

Always recognize your potential;
Cultivate a deep connection to your feelings and intuitions;
Compassion is always an option;
Love is limitless;
Live life as a spiritual process; and
Honest communication with an open heart always starts with
you.

Message from the Angel of Dreams

To think your dreams unimportant and squelch them in return is to call those who live their dreams, vain.

Message from the Angel of Trust

Needing assurances that everything will turn out right suggests an opportunity is present for you to deepen your sense of trust in your creative potential.

Message from the Angel of Time

You say you believe everything takes time, but time is only a man-made tool used for measurement. Now what? Hmm . . rethinking your excuse?

Message from the Angel of First Steps

No matter who you are, every goal in life requires a first step.

Message from the Angel of Creative Potential

Your creative potential includes choosing your thoughts, beliefs, words and actions with full awareness. All your life you have been using your creative potential for absolutely everything! At this moment, your life is the sum total of your creative potential. If you are not happy with your life now, change your thoughts about it.

Message from the Angel of Present Moment

Living in the present moment where life exists can be difficult at times. Often the struggle arises due to the conflict between living in the present moment and having goals. For many people, the thought of living in the present moment means that things will not get done without focusing on the future. This, however, is not true.

For example, if you are sitting in your living room and you decide to get something to drink, you are in the present moment. Your thirst is in the present moment too. The drink is your goal. In the present moment, you need to take that first step towards the kitchen so that ultimately you end up there. If you were to wish you were already in the kitchen drinking you have just projected into the future and created struggle. At the same time, your projection into the future has no power with which to bring to you what you want to create. Remember, life is in the present moment.

Message from the Angel of Obstacles

Obstacles often arise to assist you with generating greater clarity about what you want to create in your life. A sense of renewed commitinent or developing qualities of deeper understanding and compassion may also be some of the unexpected blessings from these challenging situations. The clarity created or the blessings received are not important. What matters most is that you find these elements within the obstacles.

Message from the
Angel of Memories

Life in the present moment sustains us, not memories.

Message from the
Angel of Soul Love

To deny your soul's deepest expression is to deny the truth of who you are. Your soul is not stingy with whom it expresses its love. It is only human nature to deny the experience and expression of love. To withhold loving because there needs to be a one and only in your life is not love. Love crosses all boundaries. It is limitless. Choose today to release the desire for a soul mate and choose, instead, to love all souls.

Message from the Angel of Attitude

It is not a question of whether the sun will rise in the morning, but how you plan to greet it.

Message from the Angel of Success

There is no such thing as failure. It is just that some situations take longer until you see success.

Message from the Angel of Dreams

Dreams may be fragile, but holding them deep within you for safekeeping is not the way they were meant to be lived.

Message from the Angel of Change

It is easy to blame Spirit or the Universe when things do not go the way we think they should. It is more powerful to seek understanding about the changes that need to occur within ourselves and our lives and then to make them.

Message from the
Angel of Service

Smile today at everyone who crosses your path for the potential
impact it could have on their life may be profound. Human
angels never know when they are going to be called into service,
especially for the humblest of acts.

Message from the Angel of Love

Love does not enter your heart when you *think* about it. Love enters your heart when you *choose* to experience it and to share it with others.

Message from the Angel of Commitment

Commitment is a very powerful word in our society that has been both used and abused by many. When disempowered, commitment can be used in a way that limits one's spiritual growth. Often when this occurs, one is coming from a perception of lack or needing some form of validation. This energy of commitment arises from the ego and can cause great struggle while providing you with powerful growth lessons. When empowered, commitment is a highly effectual word that allows one to channel their energy towards the completion of a goal aligned with Spirit.

Message from the Angel of Awareness

Awareness of yourself is pivotal in your personal and spiritual growth. Lack of awareness only creates struggle and conflict.

Message from the
Angel of Divine Love

The love you truly seek in your life is not human love, but Divine
Love. Divine Love is a state of being that is healing, joyful and
above all, always present regardless of your human experiences.
With Divine Love, there is no need for validation. You know you
are valuable. With Divine Love, there is no need to feel worthy.
You are worth made manifest. When you are connected to Divine
Love, you Are. Life becomes a process for you to hold this space
of Love for others so they may connect to Love and remember
who they Are. This is your soul's dream and it is your greater
purpose for living.

Message from the Angel of Awareness

Each day, opportunities to expand your understanding of the energetic intricacies of life present themselves. By increasing your conscious awareness of your surroundings, you make full use of the gifts and abilities you have been given. Not only will you enhance your own life as your conscious awareness deepens, you will enhance the lives of others that cross your path and those who walk the path with you.

Message from the Angel of Love

It is love that nourishes you, reminds you of your essence, chases away the fears and leads you into the wonders of creation and the experience of daily miracles. Even with all these promises of love and the magic it can weave, the fear of embracing it scares you so. You question your worthiness, your value and even if there will be enough for others should you open your heart to receive it. So how do you address all these struggles with love? Let love in. Choose it in every situation and every interaction. Choose first to love yourself and then you will be able to love others. Only love is real and you are love made manifest.

Message from the
Angel of Present

The past prepares us for the present. It is through our past
experiences that we gain inner strength and glean spiritual
wisdom that serves us in the here and now. But, understand this,
our present and future are not our past.

Message from the Angel of Wholeness

Imagine the beauty of a place where each individual recognizes his or her own importance to the greater whole. Without your individual contribution to the whole, the work of art called life remains incomplete.

Message from the Angel of Peace

Blocked by our internal desire for self-preservation, we judge those we perceive to be different as unacceptable. Acknowledging our judgments and lack of acceptance as opportunities to fortify our sense of self would serve us much better. It is only through a strong sense of self that we can truly move into acceptance of others and ultimately move into world peace. Notice, though, that it all starts with you.

In honor of the 14th Dalai Lama's speech on "Inner Peace for Global Peace" at UCLA on May 26, 2001.

251

Message from the
Angel of Acknowledgment

You are truly a powerful, creative being. Even though you may fear your creative power, it is who you are. There is no escaping it. There is only denial.

Know this: Your creative power is there whether or not you choose to acknowledge it. Again, your creative power is there whether or not you choose to acknowledge it. You cannot lose this creative power. It *is* who you are.

Message from the Angel of Willpower

Healing does not occur through willpower. It must originate from the soul and move into the physical realm of existence. To do this, you must connect with your soul first so the Divine life force within each cell can be activated and communicate with your body. Willpower, however, is required to maintain the daily connection with your soul.

Message from the Angel of Fear

Fear is a funny thing when it enters your life. It has a way of making you feel powerless. The best medicine for fear is to not even go there in the first place.

Message from the Angel of Personal Power

When you do something new and it does not work out, do you feel frustrated or powerless? What would it mean for you to assume your personal power? Most likely assuming your personal power means no more excuses for living. But you believe that not assuming your personal power keeps you safe from risking... from losing. Yet, you take risks each day. The difference being if you take them from a place of personal power, there will be a lot more joy and if you take them when you feel powerless, there will be a lot more pain.

Message from the Angel of Intention

During the creation process, a vague intention creates ambiguity in your life while a clear intention results in effortless manifestation.

Message from the Angel of Remembrance

With your dreams nurtured safely within your heart, you softly pray. "Remember me."

As Spirit whispers back to you, "Let go."

With eyes closed and hands placed gently over your heart, you whisper, "Remember me."

As Spirit whispers back to you, "Release."

With your dreams now placed in palms raised skyward for all to see, you whisper again, "Remember me."

As Spirit whispers back to you, "Surrender."

Then understanding dawns . . .
Your passion dreams the dream, your perseverance holds the vision and your courage opens you to living the dream. But, it is with wisdom that you surrender the dream's manifestation to Spirit. It is through the release of your dreams to Spirit, that the sweetness of your surrender fills your heart with peace as a smile lights up your face.

Message from the Angel of Love

Many levels of abuse occur and have occurred on this planet in the *name* of love. Even though the word love has been used in these situations, be clear that it was not love that was occurring. The abuse of love has never occurred, only the abuse of the word love.

Message from the
Angel of Self-Knowledge

How to really know love:

It is in knowing yourself, not your pain, that you know love. You have been programmed for love but it is your habit to choose pain. Self-knowledge opens you to love and self-denial keeps you in pain.

Message from the Angel of Self-Transformation

How to sustain the state of knowing love:

It is your belief in lack, the belief that love comes and goes or nothing lasts forever, which hinders the sustenance of love. Change your beliefs about love and love will change you. It will be your greatest self-transformation yet.

Message from the Angel of Manifestation

Remember, it is in unlocking one's creative potential that one creates all they desire. Clarity about what one wishes to create and trusting it will manifest are also important. The challenge in this process is to remain in love and to stay in life's flow. Do not allow the ego to run free with fear, but allow Spirit to lead the way with love.

Message from the Angel of Illusion

To live your truth requires that you say yes to life not, "yes" to the illusion of what life pretends to be or what others would have you believe it to be.

Message from the Angel of Reality

Many perceptions of reality exist in our world. Whose perception of reality is right matters little. What matters is when we need others to validate our perceptions. When we need others to agree with our perceptions, we move into deep issues of hidden agendas and control that encourages the suppression of one's individuality. So the next time you feel you need someone to see something your way, stop and reflect upon your actions. Expressing your feelings of insecurity and the need to feel validated will prove more beneficial in creating loving and empowered relationships in the long run.

Message from the Angel of Resistance

Okay so you say you never asked for this situation in your life. Yet, this situation is in your life now. Obviously there is a disconnection here. Try this perspective: If something is in your life, then some part of you invited it. Whether or not you are aware of this part does not matter. What matters now is this: Are you going to continue to resist the situation or make it work for you?

Message from the
Angel of Struggle

It is not that you need struggle in your life to know yourself, but
if struggle enters, view it as an opportunity to do just that.

Message from the
Angel of Courage

Everyone experiences fear at some time and whoever feels this
fear lets it hold them back from doing something they want to
do. Next time you feel fear arise within, look it in the eye and say,
"Not this time."

That, my friend, is courage.

Message from the Angel of Adventure

The Universe calls out to you, asking you to expand and open to worlds previously hidden. There is a yearning within to go to these unexplored realms. Your only fear is with not knowing how you will relate to others after acquiring this wisdom and insight. Then you realize that needing to know this answer reflects a lack of trust in the process of life. But, you know better than this. To walk the path of the unknown develops your inner strength, while walking a path where all the details are laid out before you holds little interest and definitely no adventure.

Message from the Angel of Denial

Denial is a funny thing. We go through life thinking we have it all together until it seems that life ambushes us. Disbelievingly, we question the situation: Are we are being singled out or victimized? When this happens, we need to take a step back and review our life situation. There is a good chance that various signs or our intuitions have been vying for our attention for some time. We, however, chose to tune them out.

We are not victims of life nor are we powerless. We are powerful, creative beings. Our denial merely points out our lack of belief in our creative power . . . thus, the supposed ambush. At least now, we know the reason for our present challenge and the focus for our personal growth. This time, let us give ourselves a hand up by releasing denial, turning to face what life is bringing us and to what we are creating.

Message from the Angel of Truth

Getting to know Spirit by knowing yourself, offers you glimpses into a higher truth that challenges all you have been taught, all you have come to believe. To know Spirit means you will have to release those beliefs, to release what has been the foundation of your life, until now. Fear may prevent you from going deeper, but something stronger than fear will pull you to understand the truth, to seek it out. Although you do not know where this path ultimately ends, walk it, you must.

Message from the Angel of Purpose

Go ahead and try living the day with no conscious awareness, pretending you are "normal" so others can remain within their comfort zones. Then, go ahead and attempt to live strictly within the confines of the physical world after you have tasted the higher spiritual meaning of life. Eventually you will realize that hanging in this limbo or living somewhere between these two worlds becomes a fate worse than death. You must leave "normal", a normal defined by others who fear what they do not understand or do not see. A commitment to your spiritual life and bringing these spiritual insights into your physical living is your purpose, a purpose you need to carry out.

Message from the Angel of Abundance

Allow your abundance and your increasing abundance to be a direct reflection of what each person can do when aligned with the highest vision for her life.

Message from the Angel of Support

The tendency when you begin to live your dreams is to fear you will not be supported by the Universe on your path. But, "the Universe" is not out there somewhere. You are the Universe and the Universe is you. This can be a difficult concept to grasp at times since everyone, at some level or another, wants to be taken care of or provided for. When it does not feel as if the Universe is responding to help you create your dreams, rest assured, the lack of response is not from the Universe. Rather, it is you who are not responding to creating your dreams. What appears to be a lack of support from the Universe is only a lack of support and belief in yourself and a present opportunity to do just that. So take a moment and ask yourself the following questions: "What do you need to do in order to believe in your dreams? What would it look like for the Universe to respond with support?" These are the questions only you can answer and your answers are the key to making your dreams manifest.

Message from the Angel of Self-Worth

When you perceive yourself as other than Divine, you begin to have questions about your self-worth. So then the question becomes one of how to see yourself as Divine when it appears as if everything in your world reflects experiences contrary to this belief? The answer is very simple. Choose it. Choose to believe you are Divine and your reality will shift in ways to reflect your belief.

Message from the Angel of Control

When you use your power to control others, you ultimately end up being controlled by them and your attempt to control others is only a reflection of a deeper feeling of powerlessness. Do not allow yourself to think that you know what is best for others, even when they want you to. Focus, instead, on empowering them to be clear about what they want and support them with it.

Message from the Angel of Spirituality

Living life from a spiritual perspective cannot be something you do only when you feel like it or only when you have time. It is not an activity. It is a way of life. Remember, you are a spiritual being in a human body.

Message from the Angel of Success

Achieving success can sometimes lead to fearful feelings. While there may always be an element of fear surrounding your success, the key is not to energize it. The key is to choose success and consistently choose love over and over again. You consistently choose fear. You are familiar with fear. You are familiar with thoughts of failure. The good feelings that arise with success make you nervous because you believe they could leave you at any moment. Just this once, choose success. Really choose it, and see what happens this time around. Chances are you will be pleasantly surprised.

Message from the Angel of Power

What does it truly mean to be powerful? The actual definition of the word powerful means to be full of power, but most people define the word from more of an emotional and ego level which often leads to fear. Power, when connected to the ego, creates fear because it is more likely one will abuse it or be abused by it. Power that flows from Spirit is pure in its intention and easily sustained. Power from the ego ebbs and flows. Power from Spirit is timeless . . . limitless.

Message from the
Angel of Boundaries

You cannot transcend limiting boundaries unless you first
identify them. Begin this identification process with your
individual belief system and your progress with transcendence
will be great.

Message from the Angel of Change

When a pebble is thrown into still waters, its ripples effortlessly extend far. When you look at changing a global situation, feelings of being overwhelmed are common. However, if you look at your own individual situation first and start there, you become as powerful as a pebble.

Message from the Angel of Confusion

In all your confusion you cannot hear Spirit's voice. So you beg, "Please Spirit, speak louder so I know it is You talking to me and not my ego stating its wishes and desires."

To which Spirit replies, "Any thought, word or action done in Love is my voice."

Message from the Angel of Connection

Deeply connected you are.
Spirit feels your pain, but why
can you not always feel Spirit's Love?
Turned away from Spirit, you did.
Turn back now.

Message from the
Angel of Completeness

All that you need in life, you have within.

Message from the Angel of Expression

You are the ultimate expression of your creative potential made manifest.

Message from the
Angel of Body

Like the candle that holds the light, your body holds your
soul. Treat it as the sacred vessel it is.

Message from the Angel of Creativity

Life's creative process only needs one thing to be complete: You.

Message from the Angel of Memories

Like your shadow on the sidewalk when the sun shines behind you, holding onto painful past memories darkens each forward step that could instead be filled with light.

Message from the Angel of Comfort

Comfort is never found in a cage.

Message from the Angel of Focus

So you say you want a life focus? How about resting each evening in the knowing that you have lived the day well.

Message from the Angel of Creativity

Your creativity is the culmination and expression of your soul's experiences. To deny your creativity is to deny your soul's existence.

Message from the Angel of Truth

Truth can sometimes come at a high price, but dishonesty, even higher.

Message from the Angel of Truth

You want to speak the truth but others do not want to hear it, as they turn their back on you with ears gone deaf. So you tell them what they want to hear as anger swells within. With truth they withdraw their love. With dishonesty, you withdraw your love. Now you wonder: When did their "love" for you become more important than self-love? No more lies now . . . only truth, only love.

Message from the Angel of Meaning

Searching for meaning,
coming up empty.
Hopelessness overwhelms.
Where to turn?
Only Silence echoes.
In the Silence,
something Greater emerges.
Birds chirp,
nature pulsates with aliveness.

Meaning is not something to be found in life.
Instead, meaning is something brought to life.

Message from the Angel of Self-Sacrifice

When does living your life for others or believing that what you want for yourself is less important than what others want for you . . . when does it end? When does your self-sacrifice become enough?

Take a closer look at your prisoner. Does she look familiar? She should. It is you. Choose to unleash your chains that have held you as a prisoner for too long. You are the only one that holds the key.

Message from the
Angel of Inspiration

When inspiration hits, there is no stopping it. To do so would
only be folly.

Message from the
Angel of Life

Falling in love with life even though you feel lacking or
incomplete is more authentic than falling in love with life when
everything is going smoothly.

Message from the Angel of Choice

Within the hunger lies, hidden from prying eyes.
Doing your best to stay safe, although the cost is high.
What to do remains unseen, and the risk, too great.
The choice is between a slow death with each passing day or
exposure of your deepest dreams only to risk failure.
Have you even thought of success as an option?
Reflecting back, how can you deem yourself a failure when you
never tried for success with something you actually wanted?
Death is inevitable either way one looks at it.
The point is, however, that life is a choice.

Message from the Angel of Inner Strength

Hanging a head in shame based on life experiences matters not. Holding a head high in the face of difficulty, though, is a mark of deep inner strength. In the end, it is not the experience that counts, but the response to the experience.

Message from the Angel of Spirit

Go ahead and live your life mentally. It is all part of the process so you can understand the inherent limitations with the mind. When you tire from the struggle and feel empty from lack of joy, maybe you will finally invite the energy of your spirit into your life. With your mind, some things are possible, but with the power of Spirit behind it, all things are possible.

Message from the Angel of Dreams

Hold yourself back no longer. Who you are is who you are meant to be. If that makes others feel uncomfortable because they do not want to see where they are holding themselves back, then that is something with which they will have to deal. Your life has become a cramped cage while your dreams hang limp like unused wings. After all, what good are dreams when you do not use them to soar to new heights?

Message from the Angel of Choice

Standing here like a stranger looking in.
How did you get here?
Who have you become?
Years have passed, yet your past still clings to you.
Your choice.
If you release your past, who will you be?
The future is undecided, but one thing you now know:
Anything is possible.
Your choice . . . again.

Message from the Angel of Body

Like falling in love,
everything seems new.
Why did you not see it before?
Always, it was with you.
Too long left unattended.
Taken for granted.
No longer.
Nourish it, you will.
It is a part of you.
A house for your soul.
Sacred.
Now you are whole,
body, mind and spirit.

Message from the Angel of Dreams

No place to turn,
no place to hide.
You stand before Spirit,
your heart open wide.
Filled with Love,
shown the Light.
Aligned with Spirit now.
Joyful.
Your dreams take flight.

Message from the
Angel of Some Day

Someday you will be peaceful . . . someday love will be in your
life. Then there were all those other promises you made to
yourself, promises still unfulfilled. Looking back, someday never
arrived. When did someday get away from you?

Make someday be today.

Message from the Angel of Spirit

When it comes to making a decision in life, do not focus on which choice you need to make. Instead, be clear about the essence of what you want to create for yourself at this time in your life. Then make the choice that best reflects this. Focusing on the decision-making process in this way often creates options that, until now, had remained unseen. Essence is of the Spirit and Spirit always offers *soul-lutions* outside of the mind's realm of possibilities. With Spirit, everything is possible.

Message from the Angel of Patience

Impatience arises when you do not trust in your creative potential or when fear grabs hold of you. The inherent gift in your impatience is the opportunity to move beyond mental energy and access your spirit's potential. Connect with your spirit's potential and then utilize your mental energy to implement it. Now your movement in life will be in a forward direction.

Message from the Angel of Truth

The gift of anger is in the opportunity it presents to release self-judgment. Every situation in which there is anger at another stems from anger at yourself: anger for not feeling valuable, good enough or even powerless. You judge yourself as less than based on the corresponding experience that creates your anger. Underlying the anger, however, is the opportunity for self-acceptance through standing in your truth, the truth that you are lovable, valuable and powerful.

Which do you choose to believe, the illusion or the truth? That is a question only you can answer.

Message from the Angel of Spirit

The spiritual battle which ensues each day between ego and spirit is only a result of the ego's fear of unemployment. *Soul-lution*: Give your ego the permanent job of establishing a clear connection to your spirit and carrying out its wishes to the fullest.

Message from the Angel of Transformation

Struggle results when we do not accept what life is presenting in the here and now. Wishing life were different, however, is not the answer. The more we fight struggle, the more we empower it. Wanting to be somewhere other than where you are projects you into the future, a future that has not yet been lived. The power of transformation is in the Now, the present moment. Only through fully accepting the present moment can we begin to transform our situation more to our liking.

Message from the Angel of Success

Success is never measured by the outcome of any endeavor.
Rather, success is measured by how you bring the best of who you
are to each and every experience.

Message from the
Angel of Silence

Take a moment to close your eyes while listening to the presence
of the Silence around you. Every sound, every noise emerges
from this Silence only to fade back into It. This Silence, is the
living energy, the Force, underlying all life. Tune in and receive a
glimpse into who you really are.

Message from the Angel of Wonder

The voice of your soul calls out beckoning you to believe in yourself, to embrace your grandeur. *You do not listen.* Then your soul attracts experiences to open you to your glory. *You choose to focus, instead, on the pain in the experiences believing they prove your worthlessness.* Sadly, your soul looks on, wondering what it is you need in order to understand just how truly special you are.

Message from the
Angel of Creative Potential

Think of yourself as a projector and your life, the movie screen.
Each belief, each thought you hold within writes the storyline for
your movie, the movie which represents both your personal
power and creative potential. Whether it is a sell-out event,
however, depends *souly* on you.

Message from the Angel of Promise

A Promise to Spirit

I promise to practice unconditional love and compassion for myself in order that I may offer it to others.

I promise to show up for life, for all of it, trusting that I had a hand in creating it for a higher purpose although I may not understand this purpose at the time.

To believe in my dreams and to encourage others to dream, I solemnly promise this to You today.

Above all, I promise to always remember that I am a soul residing in a human body and it will be the light of my soul which guides me on my path back to You.

Message from the Angel of Past

Like the storms that blow in,
Spirit arrives into your life,
leaving it in pieces.
Shattered.
You are left standing here with only sharp edges.
What do you do with them?
Then you know.
Drop the pieces.
When your hands are only holding onto remnants from the past,
there is no room for your dreams to enter.
This is, after all, why Spirit entered into your life in the first
place.

Message from the
Angel of Acknowledgment

Moving past the shadows of your fears,
The shadows of your life.
Too long, excuses made.
Too long, excuses used.
This is not where you want to be.
Yet, here you are.
Acknowledged.

Dropping the excuses,
moving towards the truth.
Unfamiliar.
Finding your way.
Some darkness, more light.
Peace.
Embracing the truth.
This is where you want to be.
Yet, here you are.
Acknowledged.

Take it one day at a time.

Message from the Angel of Life

Life's Cycle: You are born and then you die. While your birth date is known, your death date is yet to be revealed. How you spend the time between your initial appearance and your final departure is entirely up to you.

Message from the Angel of Joy

When you set joy as a goal, a goal it will always remain. If, however, you set joy as an intention for living, you will feel it completely. The difference between a goal and an intention is this: A goal is something you have to strive for and an intention means you just have to be to experience it. Which one sounds better to you?

Message from the
Angel of Release

Take a moment now and choose to let go of everything in your life. Release it all. Imagine it completely gone. Up until this point, you have been living your life for everything in it. Now, you can live your life for you while enjoying what is in it.

Interesting to view how attitudes and perspectives change once there is nothing more to lose.

Message from the Angel of Attitude

You never thought you would end up here. You always thought you would be standing over there. Looking back, when you were standing over there, you thought you wanted to be here. Now you realize it is not about where you are, but how you are where you stand.

Message from the Angel of Power

We all have the authentic power to change someone else's life.
The power, however, is not in changing that person but in
changing our acceptance of the person for who they are while
holding the highest vision for who they can become.

Message from the Angel of Joy

Struggle arises when you resist accepting a life situation in the present moment. Anxiety surfaces when you project into the future from either a past memory or a present feeling of lack. In order to transform struggle and anxiety into joy choose to say, "yes" to life and to this moment. Saying an unequivocal yes to life allows solutions to any difficult situation to become known. Now the real miracles can begin.

Message from the Angel of Gratitude

First thought of the day for a person who knows they are dying: "Thank God for another glorious day!"

First thoughts of the day for everyone else: "God, I have so much to do today; I am so tired; I don't want to go into work; how am I going to get everything done?"

Do not wait until your eventual confrontation with death to be grateful for your life. Be grateful now.

Message from the Angel of Life

When life seems to have stopped flowing understand you have chosen to stop living. Within your choice lies your solution. You only need to choose to love and live again. Do not give up on life because you are afraid to believe in it and in yourself. Release the fears that you have failed in this lifetime or will never succeed when it comes to living your dreams. Re-visit your situation. Remember your external world is only reflecting your internal world. Choose to engage in your internal world again and surely you will notice the ripple effect it carries throughout your external world.

Message from the Angel of Incarnation

When the pain seems too great and the responsibilities too heavy remember this: Each person has made the choice to incarnate into this lifetime. At the same time they have chosen and continue to choose to create each and every life experience. You are not responsible for their lives or their choices. You are only responsible for yourself and the way you interact with others, the way you love others. Honor yourself with self-love and be proud of the life you lead rather than the life from which you hide.

Message from the Angel of Peace

Holding onto the past will not allow you to make a difference now. It will not make you stronger. It will not prevent you from making mistakes going forward in this lifetime. Learning from the past, but living in the present unleashes energy to help you come here and accomplish what you want to accomplish. Choices have been made and choices will continue to be made. You are not a bad person or a bad soul because of the choices you made in the past. To try and recreate a life based on something you did right or wrong in the past are not worthy goals. Your goal is to fully develop your personal power and gifts, so you can lead others through inspiration. How you live your life inspires others to live their lives accordingly. Today make choices of which you are proud. Live your life in a way that makes you proud. Only then will you find peace.

Message from the
Angel of Life

Make your life a living testimony of all that is possible.

Message from the
Angel of Money

Many people believe money brings happiness. It does not. Money is energy, pure and simple. The power you give to or take away from money is something you place onto it . . . not the other way around.

Message from the Angel of Abundance

To attract greater abundance into your life, set your intention to do so and open your energy, your life, to receive it.

Message from the Angel of Abundance

Struggling with finances occurs when you live with a poverty consciousness. Change your conscious thoughts about life, making them abundant, and all else in life will respond accordingly.

Message from the Angel of Creative Potential

Your struggles can end today, but first you must choose to release them. Only you can make this choice. So, why are you not making this choice? You can create many answers to this question or you can make up all the excuses in the world, but what it comes down to is this: You do not want it. You do not want to make that choice.

So then the question becomes: Why do you not want to make that choice? The answer is you fear your creative potential. Yes, that is it. You fear your creative potential. Go ahead and blame all your experiences of past failures. Blame all the authority figures in your life who told you what you could or could not do. When you are finished with the blaming, when you are tired because nothing in your life has changed, maybe then you will be more open to stepping into and owning your creative potential.

Message from the Angel of Commitment

Life is not difficult. It is the way you live it which makes life difficult. Every time you choose not to step into your personal power, it results in feeling like a victim of your own life. Being a victim is never easy but owning your personal power is. Own your personal power no matter the situation and choose to stop the endless cycles of self-abuse. It does not serve you other than to create pain, and if you should choose, personal growth. Living in the Earth school environment is not about personal growth and lessons. It is about remembering who you are. How you wish to remember this or how you wish to awake is up to you. Choose awareness. Now. Awareness does not have to occur after years of meditation. It occurs with a committed choice and following up that choice with action. You do it over and over again. It is not a one-time shot. It is a daily re-commitment to your life.

Message from the Angel of Spirit

Your ego wraps your mind around thinking you need this and that in order to feel happy or fulfilled. Your spirit directs you to understanding how the choices you make are ultimately an investment in yourself. It is these choices that create happiness and fulfillment.

Index